the well-fed baby

the well-fed baby

o. robin sweet
and
thomas a. bloom, ph.d.

Macmillan • USA

MACMILLAN
A Prentice Hall Macmillan Company
15 Columbus Circle
New York, NY 10023

MACMILLAN is a registered trademark of Macmillan, Inc.

Library of Congress Cataloging-in-Publication Data
Sweet, O. Robin.
The well-fed baby. / O. Robin Sweet and Thomas A. Bloom
p.   cm.
Includes index.
ISBN 0-02-045370-1
1. Infants—Nutrition. 2. Baby foods. 3. Cookery (Baby foods)   I. Bloom, Thomas A. II. Title
RJ216.S92   1994   649.3—dc 20   94—1551   CIP

10   9   8   7   6   5   4   3   2   1
Printed in the United States of America

DESIGN BY LAURA HAMMOND HOUGH

In June of 1992, we traveled to St. Petersburg (Leningrad), Russia, to adopt a baby. Upon our arrival, we located an orphanage and found a six-month-old boy whom we adopted and named Nicolai.

Nicolai weighed only six pounds when we found him and was suffering from pneumonia. He also had rickets (a severe dietary and vitamin deficiency). His total daily food intake consisted of room-temperature tea with sugar and a syrup-laden powdered dairy substitute. He had a distended stomach, and it was obvious that he was suffering from severe malnutrition.

After nine months of a healthy diet consisting of soy-based formula, infant vitamins, cereal/grains, fresh vegetables, and fruit, Nicolai is a healthy twenty-six-pound baby.

Nicolai's recovery and weight gain are due solely to proper nutrition and care (lots of love). To celebrate this remarkable recovery, we decided to write a book entitled *The Well-Fed Baby*, which we dedicate to our son, Josef Nicolai Bloom, and to his two sisters who adore him, Gretchen and Alexis.

contents

Acknowledgments   ix

Preface by Jesse Sartain, Executive Director, Chefs in America   xi

Foreword by Keith Keogh   xiii

Baby's Introduction to Eating   1

One: Feeding the Well-Fed Baby   17

Two: Breakfast   41

Three: Breads   65

Four: Lunch   81

Five: Dinner   113

Six: Soups   137

Seven: Snacks and Desserts   159

Tips for Eating Out with the Well-Fed Baby   175

The Contributing Chefs   177

Index   183

acknowledgments

We would like to thank all the chefs and food professionals who contributed their recipes as well as their time and information. Many thanks to the following families for preparing our recipes and to the children for their taste-testing skills: Greg, Joy, and David Coplans; Tom, Debra, and Caitlin Hanavan; Duke, Julie, Mac, and Jordan Bascom; David, Bertie, Erika, and Alex Alvarez; and, of course, to our children, Gretchen, Alexis, and Nicolai. We would also like to thank the following agencies for their contributions: National Dairy Board, National Restaurant Association, Chefs in America, Wheat Food Coucil, Food and Nutrition Board—National Academy of Sciences, The American Dietetic Association, WIC Supplemental Food Section, American Academy of Pediatrics, The American Heart Association, and Restaurant Business. Our most gracious thanks to Jesse Sartain of Chefs in America for taking time out of his hectic schedule to write the preface. Many thanks to Ellen Luros and Bridget and Computrition for their assistance with the nutritional component. We would like to thank our agent, Lisa Ross, who is one of the most supportive and patient people we know, for her overwhelming support on this project. We would like to thank our editor, Pam Hoenig, and our associate editor, Justin Schwartz, who believe in feeding real food to real small eaters.

preface

When Robin Sweet and Thomas Bloom first told me about their idea for a book that would include recipes and cooking techniques for infants and small children, I must admit I was taken aback. In my relentless passion for foods, flavors, nutrition, new cuisines, and new recipes, I had totally overlooked those pallid and unhealthy portions still being spoon-fed to younger generations. Why?

Most probably I had subconsciously wanted to forget those little glass jars of colored substances called baby foods which my dear mother had lovingly spooned into my mouth to satisfy my insatiable hunger. Then through adolescence, Mom would do her best to balance my cravings for the postwar standard of steak on every table coupled with my endless imagination for fun foods including sweets, processed treats, and deep-fried everything.

My father, an accomplished chef of American and Asian cuisines gradually weaned me away from my adolescent excesses. Despite peer group and media pressures to the contrary, Dad prevailed as I found cooking from scratch using creative recipes was great fun.

Though as a young teen I was already overweight with a mouthful of cavities from earlier excesses, I became transformed for life into a lover of fresh, natural dishes. My appetite for canned, processed, and fast foods vanished for good.

My wish is that every home would raise infants and children on fresh, flavorful food made from scratch from day one. We've seen the alternative in our children who are all too often obese victims of premature heart disease and other maladies even before full adolescence.

This book will definitely put you and your children on the path to healthier, more flavorful eating habits and more family fun as your kids grow up into accomplished cooks of wonderful, delicious, healthy foods.

And hopefully the tradition will pass to the next generation and the next and the next. Never forget, your children become what you feed them.

—Jesse Sartain, Founder, Chefs in America Awards Foundation

foreword

Since the beginning of time, we have been feeding and nurturing our young. As the writers of this book make clear, the diet of infants and toddlers affects their nutritional well-being and attitudes toward food as they mature. Parents need to recognize the advantages of a nutritionally sound diet as children grow both in size and understanding. For one thing, a well-balanced diet allows young eaters to develop appropriate behavioral, motor, and social skills. During the 1950s, with the inception of processed baby foods, we followed the path of convenience rather than sound good nutrition. This cookbook is the essence of getting back to basics where food is prepared in the home from fresh products with an emphasis on nutrition and taste. In *The Well-Fed Baby*, the authors have brought together some of the finest professional chefs in our country, who are also parents, to share their successes in preparing and serving good-tasting, nutritious food to their infants and toddlers. Chefs have always focused on *taste and nutrition,* using fresh, healthy products when preparing meals for their restaurant guests, and now they share some of these recipes with you.

This book contains a wealth of information not found together in one source.

When the reader needs to know about a particular aspect of feeding young eaters, it is explained concisely and goes so far as to include examples. An effort is made to accommodate families throughout America by using well-known products that can be found in most grocery or health food stores. *The Well-Fed Baby* is designed to guide parents in their responsibilities to provide healthful, nutritious, and appealing food that will encourage the health and well-being of their children. It is a state-of-the-art work in the culinary field, second only to personally consulting with the authors. I welcome it as a parent, as a professional chef, and recommend it to all who have children and need a comprehensive reference book and cookbook for preparing food for small children.

—Keith Keogh, Certified Executive Chef; Chairman of the Board, American Culinary Federation; Manager, 1992–1996 U.S. Culinary Team; President, World Association of Cooks Societies

the well-fed baby

baby's introduction

to eating

Parents generally have the most profound and lasting influence on their children's eating habits and food tolerances. To a large extent, these tolerances and habits are influenced by how babies are introduced to foods, how we promote good eating habits, and how we educate them about food. This educational process involves more than just good versus bad, i.e., avoiding sugar, fat, cholesterol, sodium, etc., and emphasizing fruits and vegetables. The educational process should include introducing children to a wide range of tastes and textures, without a preordained dichotomy between "foods that are good for you" and "foods that taste good."

Today most adults are aware and firmly convinced that natural foods surpass processed foods in both flavor and nutritional value. These same adults know that diet and health are inextricably linked and therefore have altered the way they eat and cook. Unfortunately, these realizations have not always filtered down to the way we feed our youngest eaters.

We often fail to associate infant nutrition with adult nutrition, thinking that infant nutrition is somehow removed or distant from our own notions of healthy eating. Consciously or unconsciously, most parents associate the feeding of infants, six months to one year with the purchase of costly multicolored little jars, with each color representing variety. With confidence and trust, we place the nutritional responsibility and diet of our children in the hands of baby food manufacturers, who often charge high prices for processed foods that can be made naturally at home in just minutes at a fraction of the cost.

Today, with a soft economy projected through the mid-1990s and an increased concern for healthy eating, more families will undoubtedly be preparing most meals at home. This cookbook is designed specifically for parents and children of the 1990s.

The Well-Fed Baby presents an enjoyable, economical, and sound system of preparing nutritious foods for babies. It reflects the expertise of the two authors: O. Robin Sweet is a pediatric nurse and expert on health and prenatal and toddler care; Thomas A. Bloom is a trained chef and president of The California Culinary Academy. We have invited additional recipes from other influential chefs who have mastered the art of making healthy and delicious meals for babies and toddlers— their own and those of their customers. You will note that some of the recipes are without a chef credit and are either recipes that we have created or recipes donated without a chef's name.

The recipes originate from professional chefs and other food professionals whose cooking philosophies focus on using natural ingredients to prepare nutritionally well-balanced meals. These individuals do not bring an elitist approach to the book. Rather they have fully embraced national and international nutritional concerns and address them on a daily basis in both their professional kitchens and their kitchens at home. These chefs understand food values as well as flavors and textures and are dedicated to the principle that food, while necessary to sustain life and assure proper growth, is also a joy, a ritual, and a binding force between (in this case) babies and their families. Most of the chefs who have contributed recipes have babies and/or small children, and their recipes reflect both their personal and professional work with baby food. Each recipe is intended to be unique, simple, not fancy, easy to make, economical, delicious, and nutritious. In all, they represent *real* food for real small eaters.

This is a unique cookbook designed to add a special flair to the diet of infants. The book teaches adults all they need to know about how to introduce babies to solid foods: which foods to avoid for allergic reactions; early tolerances; quantities (portion control); and dietary balances to assure proper nutrition. All recipes are economical and nutritionally sound for children between six and twelve months of age.

In this age of low-fat and fat-free diets, some parents incorrectly believe that their babies should be placed on such a diet immediately. What most parents do not realize is that babies need fat for healthy brain development, and the majority of pediatricians feel that low-fat diets are not recommended for babies under two years of age.

Healthy eating is one of the most important things we can do for ourselves and our children. Most pediatricians recommend that infants not include solid foods in their daily diet until they are six months of age. They have found that the protein, fat, and carbohydrate content of breast milk and formula is nutritionally complete and properly balanced for babies, whereas the addition of solid foods changes this natural balance and may tend to promote food allergies. The early introduction of solids often increases the possibility that infants will develop allergies as well as increasing the sodium content of the child's diet. This may eventually contribute to high blood pressure or obesity later in life. Solid foods also interfere with the absorption of iron in breast milk. Contrary to popular belief, solids do *not* help babies sleep through the night. Also, physically, before six months of age, your baby does not have a digestive system capable of processing solid foods or the motor development to eat them, because the baby's tongue and cheek muscles have been used only for sucking. Therefore, by holding off on solids, you are allowing your baby's motor development and immature digestive system time to grow ready for other foods. After a half year of being strengthened with breast milk/formula, most children's digestive systems are mature enough to start drawing nutrients from other foods. Your baby may be ready for solids at about six months of age or more when not satisfied with extra feedings. Active babies may require solid foods a month earlier, while others refuse to swallow anything until they walk. If your baby is chewing toys out of hunger, rather than for relief of sore, teething gums (which only a parent can tell), or is eyeing your lunch, then it may also be time for solid foods.

According to the Academy of Pediatrics, six months can be an important age for a baby's nutritional needs. The iron supply that mothers give to the child before birth is nearly gone, so extra nutrients may be needed.

food sanitation and safety

When preparing and/or storing food for your infant/toddler, you should be knowledgeable about food-borne illnesses such as staphylococcus, salmonella, and botulism.

Staphylococcal food intoxication is one of the most common types of food borne illnesses reported in the United States. The symptoms are nausea, vomiting, cramps, and diarrhea. These signs appear suddenly, usually within one to six hours after the contaminated food is eaten, and they last for twenty-four to forty-eight hours. Most affected individuals recover without any complications. Though this pathogen is sometimes found in meat and poultry, human beings are considered to be the most important source. Staphylococcus bacteria are commonly found in the nasal passages and throat, on the hands and skin, and especially in infected cuts, abrasions, burns, boils, and pimples. To prevent staphylococcal intoxication, refrigerate food promptly (especially sliced and chopped meats, custards, and cream fillings) at 45°F or below; avoid hand contact with food or use disposable gloves; and handle leftovers carefully, either by disposing of them or reheating them thoroughly to a temperature of 165°F or above.

Salmonellosis results from the consumption of food contaminated with pathogenic bacteria. The symptoms are slower to appear than those of staph intoxication. The illness is marked by headache followed by vomiting, diarrhea, abdominal pain, and fever. These symptoms show themselves within six to forty-eight hours after ingestion of the contaminated food. Milder cases usually last two to three days, while severe infections may last longer and can, in rare cases, be fatal.

Salmonella bacteria are found in domestic and wild animals, including pets such as turtles and ducklings, as well as human beings. Persons who eat food contaminated by salmonella may not necessarily become ill but may become carriers of the bacteria and transmit them back to food. A multitude of foods are implicated in outbreaks of salmonellosis: meat and poultry, especially sausage; lightly cooked foods containing eggs and egg products; shellfish, especially oysters and clams; fish from polluted waters; and unpasteurized milk and other dairy products.

The following steps will help guarantee that these bacteria do not infect the consumer: 1) Avoid cross-contamination—salmonella bacteria are frequently present in raw poultry, so do not use the same utensils for both raw and cooked poultry without cleaning and sanitizing the utensils between uses. Separate cutting boards should also be maintained for raw and cooked foods. 2) Use pasteurized dry milk and eggs, and never use eggs that have dirty, cracked, or broken shells. 3) Make sure to cook food to the minimum internal temperature appropriate for each item. 4) Make sure to wash your hands every time you use the bathroom.

Botulism is a food borne illness of bacterial origin. This disease can be fatal.

Its symptoms are vomiting, abdominal pain, headache, double vision, and progressive respiratory paralysis. The symptoms usually appear within twelve to thirty-six hours after the ingestion of the contaminated food. Foods implicated in botulism outbreaks are improperly processed, usually home-canned, low-acid foods (such as green beans, mushrooms, corn, beets, spinach, figs, tuna) and smoked vacuum-packed fish. Preventive measures include avoiding home-canned foods and avoiding canned goods if the can is swollen or shows signs of internal pressure or if the contents are foamy, foul smelling, or give some other indication of being spoiled. Do not even taste suspect goods. Death can result from a single taste of botulinum-contaminated food.

We recommend preparing most recipes for one meal only. In most cases, fresh seasonal food is best. If packaged foods are used, labels should be checked and those with high salt and sugar content should be avoided. If you do have leftovers, place the food in a clean container, leave the lid off until the food comes to room temperature, and then place it in the refrigerator. Another option is to cool the food quickly by putting it in a shallow pan, placing the pan in an ice bath, and then placing the food in a clean, dry container with a lock top and freezing immediately. Freezing is recommended when storing foods longer than forty-eight hours, but do not freeze food for more than one month. Foods may be frozen in ice cube trays or small airtight containers so that individual servings can be heated and used one at a time; do not refreeze thawed food. Labeling and dating of all frozen foods are advisable. To clean the cooking utensils before and after use, please scrub all equipment with soap and hot water and rinse well. If you feel the need to sanitize the equipment, you must place the utensils in boiling water or use a sanitizer. Clean means free from food soil or dirt. Sanitary means free of germs. Some dishwashers actually have a "sani-cycle," which is an easy, convenient way to sanitize.

Baby foods may be prepared using a food processor, electric blender or food mill, or by mashing with a fork. The food that you have prepared for one meal should not be reused if you have put the spoon from the baby's mouth back onto the dish of food. The bacteria from his saliva could contaminate the remaining food. Discard any leftovers from the dish.

food allergies

Food allergies develop when a food triggers a reaction to the baby's immune system and the body reacts to the food as a harmful substance. Allergic reactions vary in degree. The gastrointestinal tract can be affected, and your baby may experience cramps, diarrhea, vomiting, and/or nausea. The respiratory system may react to a food by causing wheezing, coughing, sneezing, runny nose, or shortness of breath. Skin reactions may include a rash, hives, or swelling of the lips or around the eyes. The symptoms of an allergy may occur immediately, within a few minutes, after a few hours, or sometimes not for forty-eight hours. If you notice any of these symptoms after feeding your baby a specific food, we recommend that you contact your pediatrician. Some of the foods most likely to cause allergic reactions include: cow's milk, egg whites (though when used in larger recipes, the baby's intake of whites is so very small that it does not usually present a problem), peanuts, soybeans, shellfish, wheat, peas, beans, and certain spices. If your family has a history of allergies, also monitor your baby's reaction to pork, fish, nuts, cabbage, corn, tomatoes, citrus juice, onions, wheat, rye, yeast, chocolate, and all berries. While most babies won't have an allergic reaction to these foods, you must introduce them slowly and look for any unusual reactions.

things to avoid

Anything artificially colored, high in sugar, fat, preservatives, salt, or adulterated with additives is not good for your baby. The only sweetener you should be using is natural fruit juice. The natural sugars found in fruit, vegetables, grains, and breast milk are necessary to our diets and are processed efficiently. Added sweeteners, including natural sweeteners, refined sugar, and artificial sweeteners are empty calories and crowd out the foods your baby really needs. It is necessary to use sugar in some of our recipes, but the amount of sugar per serving is minimal. Avoid foods high in sodium such as bacon, potato chips, ham, pickles, deli foods, salt, sausages, and smoked foods. Avoid foods high in fat such as chocolate, coconut oil, croissants, fatty foods, fried foods, margarine (more than the recommended daily allowance), nuts, pastry, and salad dressings. Avoid processed foods or foods high in sugar such as candy, cakes, canned foods (check the label to see if it is packaged in natural fruit juice as opposed to syrup), flavored drinks, processed cheese, marinated cherries (red dye), condiments (catsup, mustard, mayonnaise, relish), prepackaged cookies, diabetic foods (saccharin is added to some and has been found to be carcinogenic), doughnuts, gelatins, hot dogs, instant foods, jams, jellies, processed meats, and pie. Avoid the following miscellaneous foods: citrus fruits (too acidic in the first year of life), coffee, egg whites, honey, rye bread, strawberries, and bleached white bread.

Avoid the following foods because they are not completely digestable by babies under two years of age and are known to cause choking: nuts, hot dogs, popcorn, grapes, sunflower seeds or seeds of any kind, uncooked carrots (except whole fat carrots for teething), and whole corn kernels.

a note about honey

Never feed your baby honey or use it to coat a pacifier during the first year. Honey may contain spores of a bacteria that can cause infant botulism and affect the baby's nerves and muscles, and can be fatal. Symptoms of this disease include weakness, constipation, and poor appetite. These bacteria can grow in the infant's intestine and become a strong poison. It is possible that raw fruits, raw vegetables, and corn syrups (light and dark) may also contain the botulism spores. To be safe, follow the advice of your pediatrician. If your baby develops this problem, he may need to be treated in a hospital. Almost all babies with this disease recover fully if treated in time. After one year of age, babies generally no longer get sick from eating honey. We have included recipes that use honey, but they are cooked or baked items that do not transmit the botulism.

basic feeding information

teeth

Avoid giving your baby fruit juice or milk in a bottle and then putting him to bed. Milk or juice will pool in the baby's mouth, which will promote tooth decay even before he has teeth! It is also not wise to feed him anything sweet before bedtime, as this coats the mouth with sugar. It is very important that, as soon as your baby has even one tooth, you brush it at least once a day. Use a baby toothbrush or a clean piece of gauze to wipe his teeth after every meal. Tooth decay is caused by an excess of sugar, so watch your baby's diet.

essential equipment

You will need the following furniture, kitchen equipment, and utensils in order to feed your baby.

- Sturdy high chair (try to get a tray with a lip) or clamp-on seat. Make sure that you always strap your baby into the seat
- Nonbreakable bowl and small nonbreakable spoon (coated with a soft plastic, which is preferable for baby's sensitive gums)
- Bibs, the jumbo wipe-off type, or diapers or washcloths
- Apron for you
- Plastic baby cup (with lid)
- Sharp knives to chop foods
- Vegetable scrubbing brush for washing produce
- Peelers for fruits and vegetables
- Vegetable steamer
- Small saucepans for cooking/heating tiny portions
- Spatula with handle to scrape sides of blender
- An old shower curtain or sheet to place underneath the highchair area, or square plastic protectors, available at most juvenile stores
- Baby-food grinder (portable tool for purees), blender (to puree chunky family foods) or food processor

general guidelines for feeding your baby

- If you are still nursing, nurse your baby before feedings or offer formula. This is the most important food at this time, so if baby fills up on milk and only takes a little bit of food, this is nutritionally acceptable.
- Start with one food, a teaspoon at a time, for three days or so. Watch for allergies before adding other foods.
- General rule for pureeing or simmering: one tablespoon of water or breast milk or formula per whole piece of fresh fruit or vegetable.
- General rule for freezing: Cook and puree two tablespoons of water or breast milk or formula with two whole pieces of fruit or vegetable and fill the individual slots of an ice cube tray. Cover and freeze. About an hour before feeding baby, remove as many cubes as you need and let them thaw to room temperature. Try to use them soon after thawing. Don't refreeze any food, and throw away leftovers.
- Best cooking methods: steaming, poaching, or baking. Avoid canned and commercially frozen food, if possible; at the very least, rinse off any salt or sweet syrup.
- Vegetables and fruits: Wash thoroughly and peel to remove any trace of herbicides or pesticides from the skin. Start with lightly steamed yellow squash and other bland vegetables before adding the sweeter taste of fruits such as organically grown banana. Mash for spoon-feeding, or finely chop for finger-feeding.
- Children's food generally should not have a high flavor profile, so don't add seasonings and spices. Introduce intense flavors gradually.
- Never leave a baby unattended with food. Children can choke very easily on the smallest of pieces.

how to strain food

It is very important to strain your baby's first foods. Without realizing it, many foods that have been pureed still contain bits of skin that can cause choking. Once your baby has mastered the art of eating thicker food, it is safe to strain food at your discretion. You can purchase a strainer at any discount store, cooking store, or even at children's shops. Most strainers (except for a tea strainer) have the same type of mesh, which is adequate for straining baby foods.

To strain pureed cooked foods, simply spoon approximately one tablespoon at a time into a strainer and then, with the back of a wooden (our preference but not necessary) spoon, in a circular motion gently press the food through the strainer, making sure you do not press too hard, which would allow the skin to pass through.

recommended dietary allowances

Recommended dietary allowances are defined as food substances, liquid and solid, regularly consumed in the course of normal living. A prescribed allowance of food adapted for a particular age group is adequate in energy-providing substances (carbohydrates and fats), tissue-building substances (proteins), inorganic substances (water and mineral salts), regulating substances (vitamins), and substances for promoting physiological processes such as bulk for promoting peristaltic movements in the digestive tract.

The chart below lists the recommended daily dietary allowances for children up to three years of age.

Child's Weight up to 29 pounds

Energy (calories)	900–1,800
Protein	23 grams

Fat Soluble Vitamins

Vitamin A	400 micrograms
Vitamin D	10 micrograms
Vitamin E	5 milligrams

Water Soluble Vitamins

Ascorbic Acid	45 milligrams
Folacin	100 micrograms
Niacin	9 milligrams
Riboflavin	0.8 milligrams
Thiamin	0.7 milligrams
Vitamin B-6	0.9 milligrams
Vitamin B-12	2 micrograms

Minerals

Calcium	800 milligrams
Phosphorus	800 milligrams
Iodine	70 micrograms
Iron	15 milligrams
Magnesium	150 milligrams
Zinc	10 milligrams

Vitamin C	*Vitamin A*
Cabbage	Apricots
Cantaloupe	Broccoli
Citrus fruits	Cantaloupe
Green pepper	Carrots
Guava	Cooked greens
Strawberries	Pumpkin
Tomatoes	Squash
Watermelon	Sweet potatoes

sources of vitamin d

Chances are that your pediatrician will already have your baby on a multivitamin. Vitamin D is a hormone formed in the body by the action of sunlight. There is very little vitamin D in breast milk or cow's milk. The best source of vitamin D is the sunlight. It takes only fifteen minutes a day, even when fully clothed, to get the daily allowance. The sun on your baby's hands and face will do the job.

In summary, we hope to inform parents of the importance of infant and child nutrition and to provide information regarding:

1. How and when to introduce new foods to babies and small children;
2. How to provide a variety of healthy, well-balanced snacks and meals;
3. How to identify and avoid food allergies; and
4. How to prepare meals for a family that babies and small children can eat. *Bon appetit!*

1

feeding the well-fed baby

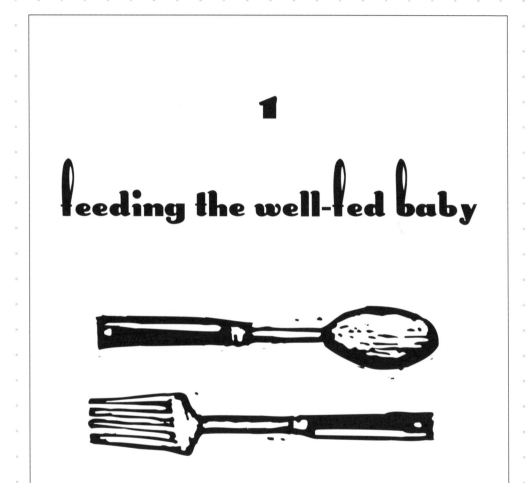

The feeding and diet requirements of babies and toddlers vary significantly with age. This chapter addresses these diet requirements by presenting month-by-month general feeding and diet guidelines for babies and toddlers six months through twelve months of age, as well as information on specific foods for babies with teeth. Baby's first bites should be diluted, just slightly thicker than breast milk or formula. Gradually increase the thickness of the mixture and the portion size as your baby becomes more accustomed to eating. We recommend beginning with cereal, then adding strained vegetables, then fruit, and finally meat. Within two or three months after your baby starts solids, his diet can consist of all of the above, distributed among three meals a day. Some parents are concerned about feeding a baby too much, but a healthy baby will stop eating when full.

simplified feeding guide on food texture

6 months: milk, cereal (strained)
7–8 months: milk, cereal, juice, vegetables, tofu and other soy food, and fruit (pureed)
8–10 months: meat (coarsely pureed or finely minced)
10–12 months: chopped foods
12–36 months: cut as tolerated

first foods

When feeding your baby, place the spoon on the top of her tongue and let her suck the food off it. Make sure that the consistency is almost liquid, otherwise she will gag. Use soft-coated (plastic) spoons so as not to irritate baby's sensitive gums.

Hint: It is much easier to feed a baby when his hands are occupied. We have multiple washable toys by the highchair that we use at every mealtime!

Every baby is different, so the amounts of fruit, formula, and cereal that we recommend are estimates. Use trial and error with your baby. We believe in pureeing one whole piece of fruit and using it in the cereal in the morning, then with tofu for lunch and dinner. It is better to have too much than too little food when your baby is fussy and hungry. Once your baby's appetite increases, one whole piece of fruit will most likely be consumed at lunch. There is also no defined time to add foods that have more texture. We find that it depends on the individual baby. Usually, you can offer "lumpier" foods when your baby has two top teeth and two bottom teeth. Up until this point, he doesn't have the teeth to grind the food into smaller pieces, so offer different foods gradually. Your baby will let you know whether he is ready for more advanced foods. The most obvious sign is gagging, choking, or just spitting the food out.

We believe in warming all baby foods to just above lukewarm temperature. Please test all foods before offering them to your baby. Microwave ovens make the food extremely hot in the middle, so the temperature on the outside is deceiving. Some of our recipes include milk, which you can substitute with formula or breast milk if you so desire. For those babies allergic to milk-based formulas, use a soy-based formula or Lactaid to replace milk. *Please consult your pediatrician before using any of these.*

We are very fortunate in California as we have a wide selection of fresh produce available throughout the year. However, this is not so for the majority of the country, so we asked our contributing chefs what they would recommend as an alternative. They suggested using frozen vegetables and fruits due to their quality and freshness when frozen and the fact that the majority of their vitamins are still intact. When you are shopping for fruit and produce, look for the very freshest, as products that have been left on the shelves for days will have lost flavor and vitamins.

feeding babies six months old

- Keep breast milk or formula as the priority food for the first year.
- Provide breast milk on request (at least five feedings every twenty-four hours) or formula (24 to 32 ounces every twenty-four hours).
- Give vitamins and minerals only if prescribed by your doctor.
- Solid foods such as cereal generally should not be started until your baby is six months old. If you choose to introduce cereals to your baby's diet before then, remember that possible allergic reactions such as diarrhea, vomiting, coughing, and/or rashes may occur. To avoid these reactions, most pediatricians recommend starting with a bland single-grain cereal such as rice, oat, or barley, moistened with water or breast milk. Wait until seven to nine months to introduce wheat, mixed cereals, high protein cereals, and cooked Cream of

Wheat. First solids should consist of the purest and most nutritious foods available. Not only are you introducing your baby to the taste of food, but you are also attempting to provide the vitamins, minerals, natural fats, and other properties of breast milk.

- When you first introduce your baby to cereal, it is recommended to mix 1 tablespoon of cereal with 2 to 3 tablespoons of breast milk or formula. Make it thin. As he gets older, you can make the cereal thicker and increase the portion to 3 tablespoons of cereal plus milk. Do not add sugar. Feed a very small amount, about ⅛ teaspoon at a time, slowly increasing the amount as he is able to handle it.

- At first your baby may appear to push the cereal back out of her mouth. This does not necessarily mean she does not like it; rather, she is developing the ability to use her tongue to swallow. Your baby is now developing a new set of muscles that were not used in breastfeeding/bottlefeeding. Nursing infants use their tongue to press the breast's nipple against the top of their mouth. This sucking reflex will actually push solid food out of their mouth. It is important to understand that when a baby does not want any more to eat, she will angrily turn her head away or spit the food all over you. Do not make a habit of pushing or forcing one more bite, as this is may start overeating habits.

- Do not feed cereal in the bottle with milk. Feed from a spoon. This further helps the tongue muscle development, which in turn helps promote clearer speech patterns later on.

- It is best not to add salt, sugar, pepper, or seasonings to your baby's foods. It is not necessary for a baby's diet, nor is it recommended by the American Dietetic Association.

At six months of age, you may start with your everyday, home-cooked whole foods. Not only will you spare yourself the tremendous expense of buying processed baby foods, but your baby will become accustomed to the taste of different foods.

As your baby develops more teeth, he will be able to enjoy a greater selection of solid foods and will make an easy transition to enjoying whatever you are eating.

At six months old, some babies are ready to plunge right into finger-feeding. To help your baby, simply place small bits of food on the high-chair tray or on an unbreakable plate.

If she seems too young for anything but spoonfeeding, try holding her on your lap and gently letting a tiny bit of food slip from the spoon into her mouth.

perfect first foods

Most babies enjoy certain foods over others. The following are foods that are nutritionally sound and safe for your baby at six months of age:

- Whole-grain toast (crusts of bread), bagels, or unsweetened cereal
- Whole-grain rice, oats, or barley (pureed or serve as cereal)

terrific teething foods

At six months of age, many babies begin teething and need foods that both feel good on the gums and meet nutritional requirements.

Bread crusts (well-toasted, whole-grain bread) and bagels are great for teething. You can save "heels" in the refrigerator; chilled crusts or bagels are often rock hard and nicely cold on baby's gums.

Carrots also work well. Make sure it's a nice fat one, and has been cleaned and peeled. Carrot sticks are too small and a teething baby might break them into small, chokeable pieces. Place the carrot in the freezer for a while, and the coldness will feel wonderful on his sore gums.

feeding babies seven months of age

- Provide breast milk on request (approximately five feedings every twenty-four hours) or formula (24 to 32 ounces).
- Give vitamins and minerals only if prescribed by your pediatrician.
- Your baby is now ready for cereal mixed with pureed fruits, and vegetables.
- You may now introduce other cereals, including high protein cereals and Cream of Wheat (4 to 6 tablespoons of dry cereal mixed with 2 to 4 ounces of breast milk or formula).
- Introduce new foods one at a time, including such foods as pureed or mashed fruits and vegetables. Begin with 1 tablespoon and gradually increase the amount given to 4 tablespoons (as tolerated).
- When you introduce a new food to your baby's diet, wait three days before introducing another. If an allergic reaction such as a rash, vomiting, or diarrhea should occur, it will then be easy to determine which new food caused the problem.
- Giving your baby a larger amount of a single food at a feeding rather than

small amounts of several foods, allows him to get used to a new food so that he will be less likely to reject it. He is also less likely to have an allergic reaction, because his body only has to handle one new food item at one time. When you serve several foods at one time, it may be difficult to detect which food caused an allergic reaction if there was one.

cereals

Iron is important, because by this time your child's iron stores are used up, and children need iron so the brain will develop properly. Over a period of time, babies can learn to accept different tastes and textures and learn to feed themselves while also developing chewing skills. Once he has mastered the technique of eating cereal, you can add foods with a coarser texture and stronger taste to the cereal, such as squash, sweet potatoes, or green beans. Mixing pureed cooked vegetables or beans with cereal provides excellent, nutritious food until she is ready for chunky, chewy foods such as broccoli or cooked carrots.

preparing your baby's cereal

At seven months she is better able to digest the cereal, and you can gradually thicken it by adding more cereal to the liquid.

Every three days, she should be ready for a new cereal and a new taste experience. A good order is a rice cereal, then oatmeal, then a barley cereal. If you use a dry cereal, you must soak it thoroughly until it is soft, then dilute it to the right consistency.

vegetables

Once your baby is eating cereals, he should be ready to try vegetables. Pediatricians recommend that you introduce vegetables first rather than sweet fruits to reduce the tendency to develop a sweet tooth. Start with pureed or strained green beans and peas, pumpkin, squash, and potatoes (both sweet and white). Then your baby will be ready for chewy vegetables; try zucchini, broccoli, cauliflower, asparagus tips, and kale. Don't feed him pureed spinach, beets, turnips, carrots, or collard greens until at least nine months of age, as these vegetables may be too rich in nitrates.

soy food

Tofu (soybean curd) is a wonderful protein substitute for meat which infants have a tendency to reject. We have included various recipes that include tofu in both the lunch and dinner chapters. Tempeh is another soy food produced by a natural aging process. Tempeh, like yogurt, is a live food whose active enzymes make it easily digestible. It also is the best vegetarian source of vitamin B-12 currently known. Tempeh is as versatile a food as tofu and has a distinctly meatier taste and texture. It can be found in any health food store or specialty grocery store in the dairy section.

fruit juice

At around seven months of age, noncitrus fruit juice is a welcome addition to the baby's diet. Dilute fruit juice with water (two parts to one) at first, because babies' digestive systems are very sensitive, or use baby juices. Use strained unsweetened fresh, canned, or frozen juices. If the juice does not come prestrained, then use a very fine sieve. Start with apple, pear, and peach juice/nectar. We recommend using the bottled infant juices because of their purity and lack of pesticides. Some apple juices on the market still use apples that were sprayed with alar, which infant juices do not use. Do not give citrus juices until your baby is one year old to prevent possible allergic reactions. Do not give artificially flavored fruit drinks such as punch or soda. These are often lacking in nutrients. To start, simply offer 2 ounces of fruit juice and 1 ounce water mixed together in a small plastic cup that has a covered top and a drinking spout, or in a bottle. Gradually increase to 4 to 8 ounces of juice every twenty-four hours.

fruit

About a month (seven to eight months of age) after introducing vegetables to your baby's diet, she should be ready to eat noncitrus fruits. Start with cooked fruit, which is softer and easier to puree; it is easiest to bake it. Preheat the oven to 350°F, wash the fruit, and bake it in its skin (pierce the fruit's skin with a fork to make sure it does not explode in the oven) in a covered dish with just a little water. When it's tender, it is done. Apples, peaches, apricots, pears, nectarines, papayas, and plums are recommended. Avoid nonorganically grown bananas, as their porous skins admit the toxic fungicides that must be sprayed on all imported fruits. If you want to serve your baby bananas, purchase organically grown bananas. Feed your baby only fruits that are in season (it is more economical and your baby is getting fresh as opposed to canned fruits) and that are washed or peeled. Buy local, ripened, organically grown fruits, if possible. After your child has mastered eating cooked fruit, introduce uncooked mashed fruit to her diet; the chewier texture will help her learn to chew.

feeding babies eight months of age

As your baby matures, you may begin to introduce new foods as well as increase the amount of food.

- Provide breast milk or formula on demand (four to five feedings every twenty-four hours) or formula (24 to 32 ounces).
- Continue to feed him cereal (4 to 6 tablespoons a day).
- Continue to feed him vegetables, cooked and pureed (4 tablespoons a day).
- Continue to feed him fruit, cooked or fresh and pureed (4 tablespoons a day).
- Provide water (3 to 4 ounces a day in hot weather or as desired). Most pediatricians recommend introducing fluoridated water at this time. Most babies tend to choke and spit on water only because it is a thinner liquid than they are accustomed.
- Give vitamins and minerals only if prescribed by your doctor.

- You may now introduce hard-boiled egg yolks. Use the yolk only. Mash the hard-boiled yolk with a fork and mix with a little breast milk, formula, and/or infant cereal. It is not wise to include egg whites in the diet before the first year, as there is a risk of promoting allergies. Begin with one teaspoon of egg yolk and gradually increase until the whole yolk is eaten. We recommend hard-boiling eggs, which kills the bacteria salmonella that can cause mild gastroenteritis (upset stomach), while other strains can cause fatal food poisoning. Please cook all eggs until they are well done.
- Cottage cheese and plain yogurt may also be offered at eight months. Begin with 1 tablespoon and gradually increase to 2 to 4 tablespoons. Yogurt is more digestible than cow's milk and adds beneficial lactobacillus organisms to the baby's intestinal tract. You can mix fresh fruit with it, but stay away from the commercial high-sugar yogurt-with-fruit combinations. Many contain preservatives, so please read the label carefully. Sheep's yogurt is another wonderful option. However, it may be difficult to locate in your local grocery; try health food stores or local farms. Your child may enjoy plain yogurt all her life if she acquires a taste for it now.
- Lean, well-cooked meat, finely strained or pureed, can also be introduced at this age to provide protein. Begin with 1 tablespoon and gradually increase to 4 tablespoons. Start with poultry, then beef, then lamb. Purees of soft-cooked beans and lentils (strained though a sieve) are a good substitute for meat, and may be given in the same amount.
- Teething foods like unsalted soda crackers and graham crackers can now be offered. Close supervision is necessary, however, to prevent the possibility of choking.
- Remember that breast milk or formula is still the most important food for

your baby at this age. Therefore, the amount of food should not be so great that he refuses the usual amount of breast milk or formula (24 ounces each twenty-four hours, at least).

feeding babies nine months of age

At this age, you may begin to introduce new foods to your baby's diet as well as increase the quantity of food.

- Provide breast milk on demand (at least three to five feedings every twenty-four hours) or formula (24 to 32 ounces).
- Give plain water as needed.
- Give vitamins and minerals only if prescribed by your doctor.
- Continue to feed your baby cereal (4 tablespoons of cereal mixed with breast milk, formula, fruit, or fruit juice). Introduce other more advanced infant cereals such as wheat, mixed grain, and high protein.
- Continue to feed your baby vegetables, cooked and pureed (4 tablespoons a day). Try introducing spinach, beets, turnips, carrots, and collard greens.
- Continue to feed your baby fruit, cooked or raw and pureed (4 tablespoons a day).
- Continue to give your baby diluted fruit juice, which can now be diluted less or as tolerated (3 to 4 ounces per day).
- Introduce pureed meats, egg yolk, mashed beans (no skins), cottage cheese, or plain yogurt (4 tablespoons or more per day).

- Continue to use teething foods (hard, dry toast, soda crackers without salt).
- If your baby has sufficient teeth and chewing skills, you may offer ground meats, poultry, or mild unprocessed cheese in lieu of pureed. Ground meat has more texture than pureed.

feeding babies ten months of age

At eight to ten months of age, your baby's dietary needs increase dramatically.

- Provide breast milk on demand, or formula (usually in a drinking cup), three to four feedings in twenty-four hours, or a total of 24 to 32 ounces each day.
- Offer water as needed.
- Give vitamins and minerals only if prescribed by your doctor.
- Continue to feed cereal (4 tablespoons or more per day).
- Continue to feed vegetables, cooked or raw and pureed (4 tablespoons or more per day). Hold off on introducing raw vegetables to your baby's diet. He does not have enough teeth yet to handle chewing stringy celery or crisp zucchini. However, you can offer soft-cooked vegetables in strips or slices.
- Continue to feed fruit, cooked or raw and pureed (4 tablespoons or more per day). You may also offer soft cooked fruits in pieces.
- Continue to offer nondiluted fruit juice as tolerated (4 to 8 ounces per day).
- Offer a choice of ground, strained, or pureed meats, egg yolk, strained soft-cooked beans, unprocessed cheese, cottage cheese, or plain yogurt (4 tablespoons or more per day).

- Continue to feed teething foods: hard, dry toast, soda crackers, or bread sticks, as needed.
- Offer plain soft-cooked pasta such as macaroni, alphabet noodles, pastina, or orzo (smaller pastas). As your baby accumulates more teeth, he will be able to handle the larger cooked pastas such as wheels, shells, and ziti.
- Begin offering small amounts of foods from the table (mashed potato, slices of soft peeled fruit).
- From ten months on, babies usually enjoy real finger foods. Give your baby bite-size pieces of peeled and pitted fresh fruit, tofu chunks, or small pieces of soft-cooked meat and poultry.

feeding babies eleven to twelve months of age

At eleven to twelve months of age, your baby's dietary needs continue to increase, and her taste buds are developing.

- Provide breast milk (three or more feedings in twenty-four hours), formula, or cow's milk (8 ounces per serving) with your pediatrician's approval (three feedings in twenty-four hours using a cup or bottle).
- Continue to offer cereal (4 tablespoons or more per day).
- Continue to offer vegetables (4 tablespoons or more of bite-size pieces).
- Continue to offer fruit (4 tablespoons or more of bite-size pieces).
- Continue to offer undiluted fruit juice (8 ounces or more per day).
- Continue to offer water as needed.

- Offer ground or bite-size choices of meat, poultry, fish (be very careful to avoid fish with bones—try tuna!), unstrained cooked beans and lentils, cottage cheese, unprocessed mild cheese, or plain yogurt (4 to 6 tablespoons or more per day).
- Continue to offer teething foods.
- Offer a variety of regular table foods, including mild casserole dishes. He may now be feeding himself.

At twelve months, your baby should be able to eat almost everything the family is eating. He should be drinking from a cup. If he rejects a certain food or beverage, do not urge him to eat or drink it. He may need time to "learn to like" certain foods. Be patient. Simply try again.

Remember, toddlers have smaller appetites. Do not become overly concerned if your one year old suddenly stops eating as much as she used to. Your baby may have gained twelve to twenty pounds during the first year of life, but will probably only gain six to eight pounds during the second year. Babies do more developing and less growing during this period. As growth rates slow after the first year, your baby's appetite usually declines.

At this point, your baby will be receiving most of her nutrition from solid foods. It is recommended that you increase the amount of protein in her diet. Tofu is an easy-to-use form of protein that is made from nutritious soybeans and is found in most grocery stores. Beans work best when combined with grains to produce a more complete protein. For a young baby, make hummus: a combination of sesame butter (tahini) and ground chick-peas. If you like, you can puree meat and poultry from your table. Fish, similar to egg whites, tend to cause an allergic reaction in young children, so offer sparingly.

foods for babies with teeth

As your baby grows, his teeth will develop, allowing the introduction of new food experiences. Some of these include:

- Beef, cooked to at least 150°F. Extra lean, finely chopped.
- Poultry, skinned, well cooked, and finely chopped
- Pasta
- Egg yolk (before twelve months of age, then use whole egg at twelve months)
- Pears, peeled and seeded. Best fully ripened and raw.
- Avocado, peeled and pitted
- Cooked potatoes, sweet and white
- Cooked broccoli
- Cooked peas
- Cooked cauliflower
- Cooked and strained dried peas and beans. Offer sparingly to avoid gas.
- Cooked spinach
- Cooked green beans
- Cantaloupe and other melons. They make great slushies when whirled with a bit of mango.

Combinations are a great way to introduce a new food that your baby may not presently enjoy. Try apple-banana, applesauce-squash, mango-pear, carrot-squash, etc. Mixed flavors can help introduce a new food, or reawaken baby's taste for an old favorite. Carrots and smooth peanut butter make a nice spread, and spinach pureed in a blender makes a tasty spaghetti topping. Other great mashed partners include sweet potato-avocado, carrot-white potato, and any combination of the above-listed foods.

By now your baby can eat almost anything. She has teeth, so she can chew more, and her digestive system can handle cow's milk, whole eggs, diluted orange juice, fish, and wheat. Your baby may want to feed herself by now, and you should encourage this as much as possible. You will still have to cut up the food, but she can pick up the pieces with her hands and put them in her mouth. By this time, she should be eating at the table with the rest of the family.

recommended daily servings

Offer several servings a day from each food group, at mealtimes or as snacks throughout the day. A complete dinner with the recommended servings for your one year old might include a cube of cheese or meat, ten peas, a few bites of boiled potato, two ounces of juice, and perhaps some fruit for dessert. Offering different colored foods is a great incentive to get your baby to eat while also offering nutritional variety. Try to serve a green, yellow, orange, or red vegetable at both lunch and dinner. If you start your toddler on crisp, crunchy salads and vegetable snacks, he will develop a taste for fresh raw vegetables.

The U.S. Department of Agriculture's new food guide pyramid emphasizes foods from the five food groups. Each of these food groups provides some, but not all, of the nutrients we need. For good health, we need them all.

On the top of the pyramid are fats, oils, and sweets, which should be used sparingly. Two to three servings of milk, yogurt, and cheese should be offered each day, as well as meat, poultry, and fish. Your baby or toddler should get three to five servings of vegetables, and two to four servings of fruits. Bread, cereal, rice, and pasta make up the base of the pyramid, and six to eleven servings per day are recommended.

What is a serving? A slice of bread is one serving, and so is ¾ cup of cereal. A bagel or muffin counts as two. A pasta dinner usually adds three. But these are adult servings.

The following eating guide will give you a *general* idea of what your baby should be consuming during an average day.

sample eating guide for the 1 to 2 year old

Food Group	Daily Servings	Average Size of Serving
Milk	4	½ to 1 cup
Meat/protein		2 to 3 tablespoons
Meat, fish, poultry		2 to 4 tablespoons
Dried peas and beans		2 to 4 tablespoons
Peanut butter		2 tablespoons
Eggs		1 egg
Cheese		1 to 2 ounces
Tofu/bean curd		2 to 4 tablespoons
Fruits and vegetables	4	2 to 4 tablespoons
Breads and cereals	4	½ slice bread
		¼ cup cereal
		2 tablespoons cooked rice

Food Group	Daily Servings	Average Size of Serving
Food Group	*Daily Servings*	*Average Size of Serving*
Fat	3	1 teaspoon oil, butter, margarine; 1 tablespoon dressing; ⅛ avocado

Here are some suggestions for a well-balanced daily meal plan for baby.

breakfast

- ¾ cup baby oatmeal and ½ mashed banana mixed with formula or breast milk to the desired consistency (usually ½ cup)
- ¾ cup rice cereal and ½ pureed peach mixed with formula or breast milk
- ¾ cup cereal of choice and 2 ounces of any baby fruit juice (apple, pear) mixed with formula or breast milk
- 1 hard-cooked egg yolk (for babies eight months or older) mixed with approximately 1 ounce of formula or breast milk
- ¾ cup rice cereal and ¼ pureed papaya mixed with formula or breast milk
- ¾ cup baby oatmeal and ¼ cup pureed applesauce mixed with formula or breast milk
- ¾ cup barley cereal and ¼ pureed mango mixed with formula or breast milk
- ¾ cup brown rice cereal and 2 pureed prunes mixed with formula or breast milk
- At every breakfast, offer juice in a spouted cup (approximately 2 ounces)

lunch

- 3 ounces of soft tofu, and one whole piece of fruit. Place in a food processor and puree until you reach the desired consistency. You can also add two half pieces of fruit for variety (for example, banana and peach, applesauce and mango)

- ½ cup plain yogurt and ¾ cup cooked brown rice mixed with formula or breast milk to the desired consistency
- ¾ cup cooked pasta, pieces of unprocessed cheese, and formula or breast milk pureed in a food processor. Serve warm.
- 2 ounces of juice or cow's milk (twelve months or older)

snacks (morning and afternoon)

- Teething biscuits, zwieback toast
- Hard carrot for teething
- Plain bread sticks (ten months and older)
- ½ cup plain yogurt
- Sourdough bread (semistale). Most babies love gumming the crust.
- Bagels (large or mini). Cut it in half, then toast, or leave whole overnight to get stale.
- Unsalted crackers (eight months and older)
- ½ cup unsweetened dry cereal (Cheerios, Kix)
- ½ banana, cut up into small pieces (ten months and older)
- 2 ounces of juice

dinner

You can add cereal to any vegetable-formula combination to make it a meal. Offer ½ cup of pureed fruit at the end of the meal.

- ¼ cup pureed cooked carrots and ¾ cup cooked brown rice mixed with formula or milk to desired consistency
- ¼ cup pureed cooked broccoli and ¾ cup high-protein cereal mixed with formula or milk to desired consistency
- ¼ cup pureed cooked Swiss chard and ¾ cup cooked barley mixed with formula or milk to desired consistency
- ¼ cup cooked brown rice, 1 ounce pureed cooked turkey or chicken mixed with formula or milk to desired consistency
- ¼ cup pureed cooked sweet potatoes and 1 ounce pureed cooked chicken mixed with formula or milk to desired consistency
- ¼ cup mashed cooked potatoes, 1 ounce pureed cooked meat mixed with formula or milk to desired consistency
- ¼ cup pureed cooked beets and ¾ cup cooked brown rice mixed with formula or milk to desired consistency

These are just a few suggestions. The following chapters go into much more depth regarding recipes.

feeding hints

- For toddlers twelve months and older, offer small quantities of several different foods at each meal, because they tend to become uninterested in eating as their motor skills increase.
- Plan desserts as an integral nutritious part of the meal, not as a junk-food treat.
- Try and limit your toddler's intake of added sugar to 1 teaspoon a day.

- After twelve months try and limit cow's milk to 16 ounces per day so your toddler doesn't fill up on milk.
- Offer small pieces of cut-up foods (one at a time) on the baby's high-chair tray, so she feels like she is participating in the feeding process.

2

breakfast

We all know how important a nourishing breakfast is; it sustains us through the morning hours. Your baby needs that nourishment, too. But not everyone is ready to eat right after they wake up. If your baby refuses food, try again later on, but don't let her wait until lunch before having the first food of the day. Again, let your toddler experiment with feeding herself. If your child enjoys breakfast, she is more likely to eat it. Remember the amounts younger children eat will vary.

All fresh fruits should be cooked until they are soft for babies up to eight months of age. Bananas are the exception to the rule and can be used fresh. Fruits can be added to cereal to give it a sweet taste. When your baby first starts on solids, just stick with simple cereals that are iron fortified, then progress to farina and oatmeal. By the age of ten months, he should be able to tolerate all the recipes in this book with the recommended recipe modifications. Recipes that call for dried or fresh fruit should be cut small enough for his eating ability. Remember to cook all egg dishes well to kill any salmonella.

Breakfast can be as simple as offering a basic cooked grain. With so many varieties of grains on the market today, it is confusing to know how to prepare each one, so we have included a cooking guide to alleviate any confusion.

grain cooking guide

Grain (1 cup uncooked)	Liquid (Cups)	Cooking Time (Minutes)	Yield (Cups)
Barley:			
Regular pearl	3–4	50–60	4
Quick cooking	3	10–12	3
Quinoa	2	15	3
Quick-cooking oats	3	10–12	3
Rice:			
Aromatic (white) 1 ¾	15	3–3 ½	
Brown	2 ½	45–50	3–4
Brown, fast-cooking	1 ¼	10–15	2
Long-grain	1 ¾–2	15	3
Medium (short grain)	1 ½	15	3
Parboiled	2 ½	20–25	3–4
Precooked	1 (boiling)	Let stand 5–10	2
Wild rice	2 ½-3	35–50	3–4
Wheat:			
Bulgar	2	10	3
Couscous	1 ½	Let stand 5	2 ⅔
Cornmeal	4	20	3–4

preparing grains

Ground grains. Whole grains can be ground fresh on the day they are to be served. Grind the whole grain in a grinder, blender, food proceesor, or food mill. We would suggest a combination of wheat, oats, and rye. Equal amounts of each can be used, or, if preferred, more wheat and oats can be used in proportion to rye.

To cook, follow the amounts and directions above. Begin cooking the cereal about forty-five minutes before serving time, because it takes this long for the non-quick grains to cook.

Pressure-cooked wheat. Rinse the wheat and place it in a pressure cooker; cover with double the amount of water. Cook twenty minutes at ten pounds pressure. Drain and store the cooked wheat in freezer for future use.

Crockpot method. The evening before, place 1 ⅓ cups wheat, rye, barley, oats, or a combination and 2 ⅔ cups warm water in a Crockpot. Turn it on low and let it cook all night. Makes three to four servings.

breakfast egg yolk

MAKES 1 SERVING

1 hardboiled egg yolk
1 tablespoon formula or breast milk

Puree the yolk with the formula until smooth. Serve lukewarm.

RECOMMENDED FOR AGES 8 MONTHS+

raw baby fruits

MAKES 1 TO 2 SERVINGS

¾ cup seeded, peeled, and chopped fruit
1 teaspoon fruit juice
1 teaspoon lemon juice water (1 quart water mixed with 1 tablespoon lemon juice)

Place the fruit, juice, and water in a food processor or blender and blend to desired degree of smoothness. If the fruit does not liquefy easily, add another teaspoon of lemon juice water. This water helps prevent darkening of raw fruits. Store in clean, airtight container and refrigerate.

RECOMMENDED FOR AGES 8 MONTHS+.

INFANTS TEND TO BE ABLE TO TOLERATE RIPE, RAW FRUIT AT THIS AGE.

cooked baby fruits

½ cup seeded and chopped cooked fruit
2 tablespoons cooking liquid from fruit or use fruit juice (apple, pear, etc.)

Step 1: Place the fruit in a steamer and steam until soft but not mushy, about 5 minutes.

Step 2: Place the fruit and liquid in a food processor or blender and blend to desired degree of smoothness. Store in a clean airtight container and refrigerate.

RECOMMENDED FOR AGES 7 MONTHS+

chunky fruit

MAKES 2 SERVINGS

1 ripe banana, peeled
2 cups fresh blueberries, rinsed and picked over
1 cup peeled and chopped peaches
½ cup unsweetened applesauce
1 tablespoon frozen apple juice concentrate, thawed

Place all the ingredients in a food processor or blender and puree or chop. Serve warm or chilled.

RECOMMENDED FOR AGES 8 MONTHS+

fruit compote

¼ *fresh peach, peeled and pitted*
¼ *fresh pear, peeled and cored*
4 *slices banana*
2 *tablespoons apple juice*

Step 1: Place all the ingredients in a saucepan over medium-high heat and cook until tender, 10 to 15 minutes.

Step 2: Remove from the heat, puree, and serve. (You may want to allow the fruit to cool slightly before pureeing to avoid possible burns.) Fresh fruit may be subsituted with canned (use fruit canned in its own juices rather than in sugar). If you use canned fruit, there is no need to cook the fruit, just puree it and serve.

RECOMMENDED FOR AGES 7 MONTHS+

cottage cheese fruit

MAKES 2 SERVINGS

½ cup cottage cheese
½ cup ½-inch slices peeled ripe banana, mango, and/or apricot
4 to 6 tablespoons apple juice

Combine all the ingredients in a food processor or blender and puree to the desired consistency. Serve cool.

RECOMMENDED FOR AGES 8 MONTHS+

tropical treat

MAKES 2 SERVINGS

½ ripe avocado, peeled and pitted
½ ripe banana, peeled
¼ cup cottage cheese or plain yogurt

Combine all the ingredients and puree in a food processor or blender until you reach the desired consistency. Serve at room temperature or cool. This mixture may be added to any cereal of choice.

RECOMMENDED FOR AGES 8 MONTHS+

blueberry yogurt breakfast

MAKES 1 TO 2 SERVINGS

½ cup fresh blueberries, rinsed and picked over, or frozen berries, thawed
1 cup plain yogurt
¼ cup cooked oatmeal

Combine all the ingredients in food processor or blender and process until smooth. Serve warm or at room temperature. Store leftovers in the refrigerator for no more than two days.

RECOMMENDED FOR AGES 10 MONTHS+

plums and yogurt

MAKES 2 SERVINGS

2 ripe plums, peeled and pitted
½ cup plain yogurt

Combine the plums and yogurt and puree in a food processor or blender until smooth. Serve at room temperature or chilled. Any ripe fruit can be used in place of the plums. Avoid strawberries until twelve months of age. Cooked cereal may be added to give it more texture.

RECOMMENDED FOR AGES 8 MONTHS+

apple-date yogurt breakfast

MAKES 2 SERVINGS

½ cup plain yogurt
¼ cup ripe apples, peeled, seeded, and sliced
½ cup cooked barley (see page 44)
2 dates, pitted
Formula as needed

Combine all the ingredients except the formula in a food processor or blender and blend until smooth. Add formula, 2 tablespoons at a time, if you require additional liquid.

RECOMMENDED FOR AGES 8 MONTHS+

chunky pear and applesauce

3 ripe apples, peeled, cored, and chopped into ¼-inch pieces
3 ripe pears, peeled, cored, and quartered
½ cup water
1 tablespoon fresh lemon juice
¼ cup frozen apple juice concentrate, thawed
¼ teaspoon ground cinnamon
½ cup cooked cereal (oatmeal, rice, barley)
¼ cup formula

Step 1: Place all the ingredients except the cereal and formula in a heavy saucepan. Bring to a boil over medium heat, then reduce the heat to medium-low. Cover and cook, stirring occasionally, until reduced to a soft sauce, about 10 minutes.

Step 2: Remove from the heat and bring to room temperature, or refrigerate until needed. Add ¼ cup of this mixture to the cooked cereal, along with 2 tablespoons of formula at a time until you reach the desired consistency.

RECOMMENDED FOR AGES 7 MONTHS+

plums, bananas, and rice

MAKES 1 TO 2 SERVINGS

1 ripe plum, peeled and pitted
1 ripe banana, peeled
1 cup cooked brown rice (see page 44)

Combine all the ingredients in a food processor or blender and blend until smooth. Serve warm or at room temperature.

RECOMMENDED FOR AGES 8 MONTHS+

peach banana oatmeal

MAKES 1 TO 2 SERVINGS

1 ripe peach, peeled, pitted, and cut up
1 cup cooked oatmeal
1 ripe banana, peeled

Combine all the ingredients in a food processor or blender and blend until smooth. Serve warm or at room temperature.

RECOMMENDED FOR AGES 8 MONTHS+

banana and barley

MAKES 1 SERVING

¼ *cup quick-cooking pearl barley*
1 ¼ *cups milk*
½ *banana, peeled and mashed*

Step 1: Place the barley and milk in a saucepan and cook over medium heat until tender, about 20 to 25 minutes. Taste the barley to make sure it is done and not too crunchy.

Step 2: Add the mashed banana, stir, and cook for 30 seconds. Remove from the heat immediately and serve warm.

RECOMMENDED FOR AGES 6 MONTHS +

millet and peaches

1 cup millet
4 cups water
¼ cup pureed peeled peaches

Step 1: Place the millet and water in the top of a double boiler, bring the water in the bottom pot to a boil over high heat, and cook on high heat for 5 minutes. A double boiler is necessary because millet will scorch over direct heat.

Step 2: Reduce the heat to medium-low and let simmer until the millet is tender, 30 to 45 minutes. Turn off the heat and let stand for a few minutes.

Step 3: Stir in the pureed peaches and serve.

RECOMMENDED FOR AGES 6 MONTHS+

fruity farina

3 cups milk
½ cup farina, Cream of Wheat, or couscous
5 tablespoons apple juice
1 teaspoon ground cinnamon

Step 1: Heat the milk in a saucepan over medium heat. When warm, add the farina by sprinkling it on top of the milk. Cook, stirring constantly, until thickened, about 5 minutes. Remove from the heat.

Step 2: Stir in the apple juice and cinnamon and serve.

RECOMMENDED FOR AGES 8 MONTHS+

cherry tapioca

Chef/Instructor John Jensen, California Culinary Academy

MAKES 3 SERVINGS

3 cups water
¼ cup infant cherry juice
¼ cup granulated tapioca
1 cup fresh, canned, or frozen bing cherries, pitted and cut up
1 teaspoon sugar

Step 1: Combine the water and juice in a saucepan and bring to a boil. Add the tapioca and cook at a boil until the tapioca is translucent, about 5 minutes.

Step 2: Remove from the heat and immediately add the cherries and sugar. Set aside to cool. May be served warm also.

RECOMMENDED FOR AGES 8 MONTHS+

breakfast rice

½ cup rice
½ cup milk
½ cup water
¼ banana, peeled and mashed

Step 1: Combine the rice, milk, and water in a saucepan, cover, and cook over medium heat until the liquid has been absorbed, 20 to 25 minutes.

Step 2: Add the banana and stir. Cook a few more minutes and serve warm.

RECOMMENDED FOR AGES 6 MONTHS+

bronwyn's favorite breakfast cereal

Chef/Instructor Mial Parker, California Culinary Academy

MAKES 2 SERVINGS

1 cup brown rice
2 tablespoons sesame seeds
¼ cup aduki beans (available in any grocery or health food store)
¼ cup millet
3 cups water
Maple syrup, brown rice syrup, or strained fruit to taste (optional)

Step 1: Place the rice, sesame seeds, beans, and millet on a cookie sheet in a preheated 325°F oven and toast, turning occasionally, until golden brown, about 5 minutes. Remove from the oven and allow to cool slightly.

Step 2: Place the toasted grains in a food processor or grinder and grind to a fine meal. The meal may be stored at this point in the refrigerator for up to one month.

Step 3: To prepare the cereal, bring the water to a boil, add the cereal, reduce the heat to medium-low, and simmer, stirring occasionally, until tender, about 30 minutes.

Step 4: Serve warm with maple syrup or brown rice syrup if desired. Strained fruit may also be added.

RECOMMENDED FOR AGES 6 MONTHS+

grits and eggs

3 tablespoons quick-cooking grits
¼ cup milk or water
1 hard-boiled egg yolk (for ages 8 months+)

Step 1: Mix the grits and milk in a saucepan and cook over medium-high heat for 5 minutes. Stir, remove from the burner, and let rest for 2 minutes.

Step 2: Mash the yolk into the warm grits. You may want to add a little more milk to make a smoother consistency.

RECOMMENDED FOR AGES 6 MONTHS+

frittata

1 ½ teaspoons safflower oil
4 large egg yolks
¼ cup vegetable puree (any vegetable pureed in a blender)

Step 1: Preheat the oven to 325°F.

Step 2: Brush a 6-inch ovenproof skillet or pan with the oil.

Step 3: Whisk the egg yolks and vegetable puree together. Pour into the skillet, place in the oven, and bake until the eggs are firm, about 45 minutes.

Step 4: Remove the skillet from the oven and let cool slightly. Cut into bite-size pieces.

RECOMMENDED FOR AGES 10 MONTHS+

one-eyed pete

1 slice bread
1 teaspoon margarine or butter
1 egg yolk

Step 1: Cut a 2-inch hole in the center of the bread. Pressing a small juice glass or jelly jar in the center of the bread and twisting will cut out the center nicely.

Step 2: Spread the margarine on both sides of the bread and brown both sides in a moderately hot frying pan.

Step 3: Place a pat of butter in the hole of the bread and allow it to sizzle.

Step 4: Crack the egg into a bowl and let the egg white run into the bowl. Retain the yolk and drop into the hole and cook until the yolk is cooked, about 5 minutes. Cover the pan to help the egg set quickly.

Step 5: Lift out carefully and cut into bite-size pieces.

RECOMMENDED FOR AGES 10 MONTHS+

scrambled tofu

2 ounces firm tofu
1 ½ teaspoons olive oil

Step 1: Mash the tofu in a small bowl.

Step 2: In a skillet, heat the olive oil over medium-high heat. When it starts to sizzle, add the mashed tofu and, as you would with an egg, scramble the tofu in the pan with a wooden spatula or fork for about 2 minutes.

RECOMMENDED FOR AGES 10 MONTHS+

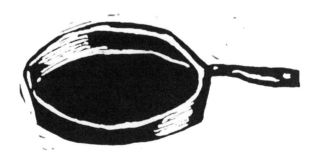

3
breads

The USDA's new food guide pyramid suggests that bread, cereal, rice, and pasta should be the basics of our diet. It also recommends that we have six to eleven servings from this group per day. The following bread, muffin, biscuit, and polenta recipes are some of the tastiest that we have ever found and have adult-size servings.

blueberry breakfast popovers

Bert Cutino, Co-owner, Sardine Factory

MAKES 10 TO 12 POPOVERS

1 ⅓ cups unbleached flour
2 teaspoons sugar
1 cup milk
1 large egg
1 ½ large egg whites
1 cup fresh blueberries, rinsed and picked over

Step 1: Preheat the oven to 450°F.

Step 2: Combine the flour and sugar and set aside.

Step 3: Combine the milk, egg, and egg whites in a bowl and whisk until blended. Gradually add the flour mixture and stir until just homogeneous. Don't overstir the mixture or it won't rise properly. Add the blueberries.

Step 4: Place the popover pan in the oven for 3 minutes. Remove and coat with cooking spray or margarine.

Step 5: Divide the popover mixture into the pans and bake for 10 minutes. Reduce the heat to 350°F and bake until golden brown, about 25 minutes. Remove from the pan and serve immediately. Cut into bite-size pieces.

RECOMMENDED FOR AGES 10 MONTHS+

oatmeal shortbread biscuits

Phyllis Bologna, Executive Chef for National Accounts Development, General Foods USA Foodservice Division

1 cup unbleached flour
1 tablespoon sugar
1 teaspoon baking powder
½ teaspoon salt
2 cups quick-cooking rolled (old-fashioned) oats
½ cup (1 stick) unsalted butter, softened and cut into small pieces
½ cup milk

Step 1: Sift together the flour, sugar, baking powder, and salt in a mixing bowl. Add the oats, then cut in the butter using a pastry cutter or two knives until the mixture is crumbly.

Step 2: Gradually add the milk, stirring until a dough is formed.

Step 3: Roll the dough out to an ⅛-inch thickness or, if you have an eager pair of small hands available, let them pat out the dough. Cut into irregular squares.

Step 4: Bake on a greased cookie sheet in a preheated 375°F oven until lightly browned, 12 to 15 minutes. Serve at room temperature. Cut into bite-size pieces.

RECOMMENDED FOR AGES 10 MONTHS+

BREADS
69

zwieback

Chef/Instructor Bo Friberg, California Culinary Academy

MAKES SEVENTY 5- BY 2 ½- BY ¾-INCH CRACKERS

Yes, this is a large recipe, but zwieback keeps well in an airtight container, and you never want to run out. The brushing on of the potato starch solution will add color and shine to the crust, but feel free to leave it out if you wish.

FOR THE SPONGE
2 ounces fresh compressed yeast
2 cups warm milk
3 ¾ cups unbleached flour

FOR THE DOUGH
1 cup warm milk
¾ cup sugar
1 teaspoon salt
3 large eggs
8 ¾ cups unbleached flour
10 tablespoons (1 ¼ sticks) unsalted butter
Potato Starch Solution (recipe follows; optional)

Step 1: To make the sponge, dissolve the yeast in the milk, then stir in the flour, mixing until you have a smooth paste.

Step 2: Cover and let stand in a warm place until the sponge has risen to its maximum volume; when the sponge is fully mature it first begins to bubble on the surface and then gradually starts to fall. This takes approximately 30 minutes.

Step 3: To make the dough, add the remaining milk, the sugar, salt, and eggs. Hold back a handful of the remaining flour and incorporate the rest. Knead in the butter and enough of the reserved flour to make a very firm dough. Continue to knead until the dough is smooth and elastic, about 6 minutes using an electric mixer on low speed, 12 minutes if you are kneading by hand.

Step 4: Place the dough in a lightly oiled bowl, turn the dough over to coat both sides with oil, cover, and let rise in a warm place until double in volume, 30 to 60 minutes.

Step 5: Punch the dough down, then cover and let rise again until doubled in volume. Punch the dough down and let it rise once more for a total of three risings.

Step 6: Divide the dough into three equal pieces. Pound and roll each piece into a 16-inch rope. Cut each rope into twelve equal pieces. Form the small pieces into mini loaves. Place the pieces side by side on sheet pans lined with baking paper. Let rise to just under one and one half times the original size, about 30 minutes. Brush the potato starch solution over the loaves.

Step 7: Bake in a preheated 400°F until completely baked through, about 25 minutes. Remove from the oven and brush again with the potato starch mixture. Set the zwieback loaves aside at room temperature until the following day.

Step 8: Cut the loaves lengthwise into ¾-inch-thick slices. Place the slices, cut side down, on sheet pans lined with baking paper.

Toast the slices in a preheated 325°F until they are light golden brown on top, about 20 minutes. Turn the slices over and continue baking until golden brown on the second side as well, about 20 minutes longer. Adjust the oven temperature if necessary; if the oven is too hot the zwieback will not have a chance to dry properly in the center by the time they are brown on the outside, which will cause them to become chewy after just a few days of storage. Properly baked and stored in airtight containers, they will stay crisp for many weeks.

RECOMMENDED FOR AGES 6 MONTHS+

potato starch solution

1 cup cold water
*¼ cup potato starch (available in the specialty section of grocery store,
    with the kosher foods)*

Stir the water into the potato starch. Heat, stirring constantly to just under boiling.

sturdy teething biscuits

MAKES 24 BISCUITS

1 tablespoon uncooked oatmeal
1 cup unbleached flour
1 tablespoon soy flour (may be purchased at any health food store)
1 tablespoon wheat germ
1 tablespoon dry milk
1 large egg yolk, beaten
3 tablespoons honey
1 teaspoon pure vanilla extract
1 ½ tablespoons canola oil
¼ cup milk

Step 1: Preheat the oven to 350°F.

Step 2: Blend the dry ingredients together in a large bowl.

Step 3: Blend the liquid ingredients together, then stir them into the dry mixture. The dough should be stiff.

Step 4: Roll the dough out thinly, about ¼ inch in thickness, on a floured surface and cut into finger-length rectangles or desired shapes.

Step 5: Bake on an ungreased cookie sheet until lightly browned, about 15 minutes. Cool and store in an airtight container.

RECOMMENDED FOR 8 MONTHS+

Please, never leave infants unattended when they are eating. Occasionally, they are able to bite off chunks, which they can easily choke on.

chef rachel's bagels

2 packages active dry yeast
4 ¼ to 4 ½ cups sifted unbleached flour
1 ½ cups lukewarm water
¼ cup sugar
1 tablespoon salt

Step 1: In a large mixing bowl, combine the yeast and 1 ¾ cups of the flour.

Step 2: Combine the water, 3 tablespoons of the sugar, and the salt. Add to the yeast mixture. Beat at low speed with an electric mixer for 30 seconds, scraping the sides constantly. Beat 3 minutes at high speed.

Step 3: By hand, stir in enough of the remaining flour to make a moderately stiff dough. Turn out onto a lightly floured board and knead until smooth, 5 to 8 minutes. Cover with a clean kitchen cloth and let rise 20 minutes.

Step 4: In a large kettle, combine a gallon of water and the remaining 1 tablespoon of sugar; bring to a boil. Reduce the heat to medium, simmering.

Step 5: Preheat the oven to 375°F.

Step 6: Take about one handful of dough and roll it with the palms of your hands into a long tube about 1 inch thick, and attach each end of the tube to make a circle (it should look like a doughnut).

Step 7: Place four to five bagels, one at a time, into the water and allow them to simmer for 7 minutes, turning each bagel once. Remove the bagels from the water, shake off excess water, and place them on an ungreased baking sheet.

Step 8: Bake until golden brown, 30 to 35 minutes.

RECOMMENDED FOR AGES 8 MONTHS+. INITIALLY OFFER BAGELS FROZEN OR STALE FOR TEETHING PURPOSES.

graham crackers

MAKES 2 DOZEN

1 cup graham or whole wheat flour
1 cup unbleached flour
1 teaspoon baking powder
¼ cup (½ stick) margarine, softened
½ cup honey
¼ cup milk (plus 2 tablespoons for glossing)

Step 1: Preheat the oven to 400°F.

Step 2: Combine the flours and baking powder. Add the margarine, honey, and milk. Blend well.

Step 3: Roll out the dough to ½-inch thickness and cut into squares. Prick with a fork, then brush with the milk.

Step 4: Bake on an ungreased baking sheet until golden brown, about 18 minutes. If rolled thicker, these crackers can be used as teething biscuits.

RECOMMENDED FOR AGES 10 MONTHS+

banana bread sticks

1 ¾ cup unbleached flour
2 teaspoons baking powder
½ teaspoon baking soda
¼ cup firmly packed brown sugar
½ cup canola oil
2 large eggs
1 cup mashed banana

Step 1: Preheat the oven to 350°F.

Step 2: Combine the flour, baking powder, and baking soda.

Step 3: In a separate bowl, cream together the sugar, oil, and eggs, then add the mashed banana and slowly mix in the dry ingredients. Do not beat or overmix.

Step 4: Pour the mixture into a greased loaf pan and bake until a wooden skewer inserted into the loaf comes out clean, about 1 hour.

Step 5: Cool in the pan for about 15 minutes, then remove from the pan and allow to cool for an aditional 20 minutes on a wire rack. Preheat the oven to 150°F.

Step 6: Slice the loaf into ¼ to ⅜-inch slices, then cut each slice into about four ½-inch-wide sticks. Spread the bread sticks out on an ungreased cookie sheet and bake until they are hard and crunchy, about 1 hour. Store in a tightly covered container.

RECOMMENDED FOR AGES 10 MONTHS+

bunny muffins

MAKES 24 SMALL MUFFINS

¾ *cup safflower oil*
¾ *cup firmly packed brown sugar*
2 *large eggs*
¾ *cup whole wheat flour*
¼ *cup unbleached flour*
½ *teaspoon baking powder*
¼ *teaspoon baking soda*
½ *teaspoon salt*
1 *teaspoon ground cinnamon*
1 ½ *cups grated or pureed carrots*

Step 1: Preheat the oven to 350°F. Lightly grease a small muffin tin.

Step 2: Cream the oil and brown sugar together until well mixed. Add the eggs one at a time, beating well after each addition.

Step 3: In a separate bowl or on waxed paper, mix together the flour, baking powder, baking soda, salt, and cinnamon. Add the flour mixture to the egg mixture and beat well. Add the carrots and mix well.

Step 4: Spoon the batter into the tins. Bake until golden brown, about 40 minutes. Cut into bite-size pieces.

RECOMMENDED FOR AGES 10 MONTHS+

pumpkin muffins

1 ½ cups unbleached flour
½ cup sugar
2 teaspoons baking powder
1 teaspoon ground cinnamon
½ teaspoon ground ginger
¼ teaspoon ground cloves
1 large egg, slightly beaten
½ cup milk
½ cup canned solid pack pumpkin
¼ cup (½ stick) margarine, melted
2 ½ teaspoons sugar mixed with ½ teaspoon ground cinnamon

Step 1: Preheat the oven to 400°F.

Step 2: Sift together the first six ingredients in a large bowl.

Step 3: In a separate bowl, combine the egg, milk, pumpkin, and melted margarine.

Step 4: Add the wet ingredients to the sifted mixture, mixing only until combined. Fill the greased muffin tins two thirds full; sprinkle with the cinnamon sugar.

Step 5: Bake until golden brown, 20 to 25 minutes. Cut into bite-size pieces.

RECOMMENDED FOR AGES 10 MONTHS+

apple-orange muffins

1 cup whole wheat flour
1 cup unbleached flour
2 teaspoons baking soda
1 ¼ teaspoons baking powder
¼ cup dry milk
¼ cup frozen apple juice concentrate, thawed
¼ cup frozen orange juice concentrate, thawed
Juice of 2 oranges (this is okay for infants because it is such a small amount)
½ cup water
2 large eggs

Step 1: Preheat the oven to 350°F. Grease a muffin tin.

Step 2: In a large bowl, blend the flours, baking soda, baking powder, and dry milk together.

Step 3: Stir in the juice concentrates, orange juice, and water. Add the eggs and blend until smooth.

Step 4: Pour the batter into the tins, filling each about two thirds full. Bake until the muffins pull away from the sides of the pan or spring back when slightly pressed, 12 to 15 minutes. Cut into bite-size pieces.

Recommended for ages 10 months+

basic polenta

Chef/Owner Lidia Bastianich, Felidia Ristorante

4 cups water
1 tablespoon unsalted butter
1 bay leaf
2 teaspoons coarse salt
1 ½ cups coarse yellow cornmeal

Step 1: In a medium-size cast-iron saucepan or other heavy pot, bring all the ingredients except the cornmeal to simmer over medium heat.

Step 2: Very slowly, begin to sift the cornmeal into the pan through the fingers of one hand, stirring constantly with a wooden spoon or whisk. Gradually sift the remaining meal into the pan, continue to stir, and reduce the heat to medium-low. Stir until the polenta is smooth and thick and pulls away from the sides of the pan as it is stirred, about 30 minutes.

Step 3: Discard the bay leaf, pour the polenta into a serving bowl or onto a wooden board, and allow it to rest 10 minutes. To serve from the bowl, dip a large spoon into water and scoop the polenta onto individual dishes, dipping the spoon into the water between scoops. To serve from the board, cut the polenta into segments with a thin, taut string or knife and transfer to plates with a spatula or cake knife.

RECOMMENDED FOR AGES 10 MONTHS+

4

lunch

ost parents notice that their children tend to eat more at lunch than at dinnertime, so it is very important to offer a well balanced luncheon menu. Try to offer one item per food group, and don't be upset if your baby tries only a little from each. This is perfectly normal. Cheese tends to be a big favorite at lunchtime, and we encourage parents to offer natural cheese as opposed to processed. Read the ingredients on both kinds of packages, and we think that you will agree that natural is better. According to the American Academy of Pediatrics, properly strained homemade foods are nutritionally equivalent if not superior to commercially prepared foods. Carrot juice can be used to replace sugar. For variety, flavor and fun, beet juice and carrot juice can be added to mashed potatoes to make rainbow potatoes. We have found that pureed green beans and peas mix better when added to a combination of cereal and formula. When mixed with just the formula, the texture is too chunky for a new eater. The following recipes are in infant proportions. Here are some fun and exciting ways to prepare your baby's lunch.

legumes (beans, peas, lentils)

1 cup any dried legume
3 cups water
¾ cup milk

Step 1: Rinse the legumes. Soak in water to cover overnight or bring to boil for 2 minutes, cover, and allow to sit for 2 hours.

Step 2: Drain the legumes, then combine with the water in a saucepan, bring to a boil, reduce the heat to medium-low, and simmer until tender. There can be a wide range in times: for example, lima beans will take 1 hour, black-eyed peas 30 minutes.

Step 3: When the legumes are soft, remove them from the heat, drain off all the remaining water and, if you prefer, puree them in a food mill or blender, or mash with a fork. Add the milk to thin. Press through a sieve to remove any pulp. Place the legumes in small containers or in a divided ice cube tray and freeze until needed. One serving is about 2 tablespoons.

RECOMMENDED FOR AGES 7 MONTHS+

cooked vegetables

A variety of vegetables can be prepared. Some good choices are green beans, peas, squash, carrots, spinach, or sweet potatoes.

¼ cup water
1 cup vegetable pieces, peeled if necessary and cut into ½-inch pieces

Bring the water to a boil in a small saucepan. Add the vegetables and steam over medium-low heat until tender, about 5 minutes. Blend or puree until smooth, adding cooking liquid or formula as needed. Let cool and use immediately or freeze the remaining vegetables.

RECOMMENDED FOR 7 MONTHS+

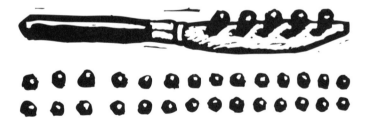

steamed veggies

½ cup shredded carrots
½ cup peeled and shredded beets
½ cup peeled and shredded turnips
½ cup red bell pepper strips

Step 1: Steam the vegetables until tender, about 8 minutes. Reserve the steaming water.

Step 2: Transfer to a blender, food processor, or food mill and puree. Use the liquid from steaming to achieve a smooth consistency.

RECOMMENDED FOR AGES 7 MONTHS +

beets and barley

1 cup water
3 medium-size beets, peeled and sliced
¼ cup cooked barley (see page 44)

Step 1: Pour the water into a saucepan fitted with a steamer basket and bring to a boil.

Step 2: Place the sliced beets in the steamer basket, cover, and steam until tender, about 10 minutes.

Step 3: Place the beets in a blender, add 1 tablespoon of water, and puree. Add more water until you have the desired consistency.

Step 4: Add the cooked barley to the beets for a complete lunch. Serve warm or at room temperature.

RECOMMENDED FOR AGES 7 MONTHS +

carrots and beets with apple

2 medium-size carrots, thinly sliced
2 small beets, peeled, cooked in water to cover until tender, and diced
½ apple, peeled, cored, and diced
⅓ cup unsweetened apple juice

Step 1: Simmer the carrots, beets, and apple in a saucepan over medium-low heat in the apple juice until tender, about 10 minutes.

Step 2: Puree in a food processor, food mill, or blender and serve warm or at room temperature. Add ½ cup of any cooked grain if desired.

RECOMMENDED FOR AGES 7 MONTHS +

carrot puree with mint

Chef Kenneth C. Wolfe, Wolfe's Cooking School

MAKES 2 SERVINGS

1 tablespoon butter
½ pound young carrots, thinly sliced
½ teaspoon sugar
Several fresh mint leaves

Step 1: Melt the butter in a skillet, then add the carrots, sugar, mint leaves, and a few drops of water. Cover tightly and stew over low heat until the carrots are tender, about 15 minutes.

Step 2: Remove the mint leaves, then place the carrots and their juice in a food processor or blender and pulse quickly into a fine puree, or mash them with a fork for older infants. Check for taste and keep warm until serving.

RECOMMENDED FOR AGES 7 MONTHS+

carrot apple puree

1 carrot, sliced
1 apple, peeled, cored, and sliced
2 tablespoons formula
½ teaspoon butter
3 ounces soft tofu

Step 1: Steam the carrot slices for 5 minutes and then add the apple slices and steam until both are tender, about 5 minutes.

Step 2: Place all the ingredients in a food processor, food mill, or blender and puree until smooth.

RECOMMENDED FOR AGES 7 MONTHS+

baby carrots and brown rice

MAKES 1 ½ CUPS

1 cup water
3 to 4 large carrots, sliced ½ inch thick
About ¼ cup formula or water
¼ cup cooked brown rice (see page 44) or 3 ounces soft tofu

Step 1: Bring the water to a boil in a saucepan fitted with a steamer basket.

Step 2: Add the carrots to the steamer, cover, and steam until tender, about 10 minutes.

Step 3: Place the carrots in a blender or food processor, add the formula, and puree. Add more water or formula until you reach the desired consistency. Add the brown rice to make a complete meal.

RECOMMENDED FOR AGES 7 MONTHS+

chick-pea puree and barley

2 cups cooked chick-peas
3 tablespoons formula
¼ cup cooked barley (see page 44)

Place all the ingredients in a food processor, blender, or food mill and process until smooth. Add more formula to achieve the consistency your baby can tolerate.

RECOMMENDED FOR AGES 8 MONTHS+

corn and butternut squash

½ ear corn or ½ cup frozen corn
½ cup butternut squash, peeled and cut into bite-size pieces
¼ cup formula

Step 1: Steam the ear of corn for 7 minutes, then cut the kernels from the husk. If using frozen corn, steam until the kernels are tender, 2 to 3 minutes.

Step 2: Steam the squash until soft, 5 to 8 minutes.

Step 3: Combine the corn and squash and half of the formula in a food processor, food mill, or blender and process until smooth. Add more formula until you reach the desired consistency. Serve warm or at room temperature. You can add 3 ounces of pureed soft tofu to make a complete lunch.

RECOMMENDED FOR AGES 7 MONTHS+

baked acorn squash and brown rice

MAKES 2 SERVINGS

1 acorn or butternut squash
2 tablespoons butter
½ cup cooked brown rice (see page 44)
½ cup formula

Step 1: Preheat the oven to 350°F.

Step 2: Scrub the squash, cut it in half, and scoop out the seeds. Place skin side up in an ovenproof dish containing 1 inch of water. Place in the oven and bake until tender, about 1 hour. You can also cook the squash on the high setting in a microwave for 20 minutes.

Step 3: Remove the flesh from the shells and place in a food processor, food mill, or blender. Add the rice and 2 tablespoons of the formula and puree until smooth. Add additional formula 1 tablespoon at a time until you achieve the desired consistency.

RECOMMENDED FOR AGES 7 MONTHS+

eggplant and couscous

1 cup water
1 medium-size eggplant, peeled and cut into ½-inch pieces
1 cup cooked couscous (see page 44)

Step 1: Bring the water to a boil in a saucepan fitted with a steamer, then add the eggplant pieces and steam until tender, 10 to 15 minutes.

Step 2: Puree the eggplant and water in a food processor, food mill, or blender.

Step 3: Add the couscous and puree again. Serve warm or at room temperature.

RECOMMENDED FOR AGES 7 MONTHS+

peas and brown rice

1 cup frozen or fresh peas, cooked in water until tender
1 cup cooked brown rice (see page 44)
½ cup formula

Step 1: Combine the peas, rice, and ¼ cup of the formula in a food processor, blender, or food mill and blend until smooth. If the consistency is too thick, add more formula 2 tablespoons at a time until you reach the desired consistency.

Step 2: Serve warm or at room temperature. Store leftovers in refrigerator for no more than 2 days.

RECOMMENDED FOR AGES 7 MONTHS+

sweet potato and apple puree

MAKES 2 SERVINGS

1 small sweet potato or yam, peeled and sliced
½ apple, peeled, cored, and sliced
2 tablespoons formula
½ teaspoon butter

Step 1: Steam the sweet potato for 5 minutes, then add the apple slices and steam until both are tender, an additional 5 minutes.

Step 2: Place all the ingredients in a food processor, food mill, or blender and process until smooth. You may need to add more formula for a more liquid consistency.

RECOMMENDED FOR AGES 7 MONTHS+

bibby's red beans and ham

Executive Chef/Owner Suzette Gresham-Tognetti,
Ristorante Acquerello

MAKES 2 SERVINGS

½ pound dried red beans
¼ pound cooked ham, diced
3 ½ cups cold water
1 bay leaf
½ small onion, diced
1 clove garlic, peeled
1 ½ teaspoons sugar

Step 1: Put all the ingredients together in a pot. Bring to a boil. Once it has come to a boil, turn off the heat and allow to sit for 1 hour. (The beans will plump.)

Step 2: Turn the heat to medium and gently simmer until the beans are tender, about 30 minutes. Remove the bay leaf and puree the mixture in a food processor or blender.

RECOMMENDED FOR AGES 8 MONTHS +

vegetarian chili beans

1 cup dried kidney beans
3 ½ cups water
½ cup chopped onion
½ cup chopped celery
1 ¼ cups fresh or canned tomatoes, seeded, peeled, and chopped
1 garlic clove, peeled
¼ cup cooked brown rice (see page 44)

Step 1: Soak the beans in 3 cups of the water overnight.

Step 2: Drain the beans, transfer to a casserole dish, and bake until tender in a preheated 250°F oven, about 3 ½ hours.

Step 3: Combine the remaining ½ cup water, the onion, and celery in a saucepan and cook over medium heat until tender, about 20 minutes. Add them to the beans.

Step 4: Add the tomatoes and garlic and simmer over low heat for 30 minutes. Puree. Add the cooked brown rice and puree again.

RECOMMENDED FOR AGES 10 MONTHS+

refried beans

2 tablespoons olive oil
*½ pound dried pinto beans, cooked according to package instructions, drained but
cooking liquid reserved, or one 15-ounce can pinto beans, drained but the liquid
reserved*

Step 1: Heat the oil over medium heat in a heavy skillet, then add the beans.
As the beans simmer, mash them with a potato masher and stir. Add reserved liquid several tablespoons at a time to achieve desired consistency. Simmer about 20
minutes, stirring occasionally.

Step 2: Transfer the beans to a food processor, food mill, or blender and puree.
Strain through a sieve to remove the bean skins. Serve warm or at room temperature. You may add ½ cup of a cooked grain and formula to make a complete protein
meal.

RECOMMENDED FOR AGES 7 MONTHS+

hippie burger

1 cup uncooked brown rice
1 ¼ cups dried lentils
4 cups water
Olive oil as needed

Step 1: Combine the rice, lentils, and water in a pot. Bring to a boil, then reduce the heat to very low. Cook until really mushy, about 30 minutes. You want it to look pretty wet, so if it looks dry don't be afraid to add more water.

Step 2: Remove from the heat and let cool in the refrigerator.

Step 3: Mush the mixture with your hands and make into individual patties.

Step 4: Heat a little olive oil in a skillet over medium-high heat. Add the burgers several at a time and cook them until browned on each side, about 5 minutes per side. Puree or chop them in a food processor.

RECOMMENDED FOR AGES 8 MONTHS+

tabbouleh salad

¼ cup finely cracked wheat (bulgur)
½ cup fresh parsley, minced
1 cup peeled, seeded, and chopped fresh tomatoes
¼ cup fresh lemon juice
2 tablespoons finely chopped green onions (scallions)
¼ cup olive oil

Step 1: Soak the cracked wheat for 10 minutes in enough water to cover. Drain and squeeze as dry as possible in a clean towel.

Step 2: Place the wheat in a large bowl. Add the remaining ingredients and mix well. Let stand for 30 minutes to allow the flavors to blend.

Step 3: Puree or finely chop if the consistency is too lumpy for your baby.

RECOMMENDED FOR AGES 10 MONTHS+

rice congee

Chef Martin Yan, Yan Can Cook

MAKES 6 TO 8 SERVINGS

1 ¼ cups uncooked long grain rice
4 thin slices peeled fresh ginger
12 cups chicken broth
½ pound boneless skinless chicken breast or firm tofu, julienned

Step 1: Combine the rice, ginger, and broth in a large pot and bring to a boil. Cover, reduce the heat to medium-low, and simmer, stirring occasionally, until the rice becomes very soft and creamy, about 1 ½ hours.

Step 2: Remove the ginger slices. Add the chicken and simmer until cooked through, about 8 minutes more, stirring occasionally. Puree or chop in a food processor if your baby cannot handle the thick consistency.

RECOMMENDED FOR AGES 10 MONTHS+

california chicken

1 whole large skinless, boneless chicken breast, cooked and shredded
½ cup refried beans (see page 100)
½ large avocado, peeled, pitted, and sliced
½ large tomato, peeled, seeded, and chopped
2 tablespoons shredded Monterey jack cheese
½ cup plain yogurt

Mix all the ingredients together in a bowl and puree in a food processor, blender, or food mill. Serve cool or at room temperature. Refrigerate leftovers and serve within 24 hours.

RECOMMENDED FOR AGES 8 MONTHS+

wehoni rice and chicken

1 cup wehoni rice (can be purchased at most health food stores)
2 ½ cups water
2 cups cubed cooked chicken
About ¼ cup chicken stock (see page 140) or formula

Step 1: Combine the rice and water in large saucepan, cover, and bring to a boil, then reduce the heat to medium-low and simmer until tender, about 45 minutes. Rinse the rice in hot water; drain well.

Step 2: Combine the rice and chicken. Add the chicken stock and puree.

RECOMMENDED FOR AGES 8 MONTHS+

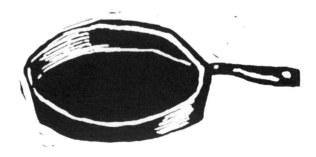

monkey sandwich

¼ cup natural smooth peanut butter
2 slices bread
½ medium-size ripe banana, peeled and sliced ½ inch thick

Step 1: Spread the peanut butter on the bread.

Step 2: Place the banana slices on top of the peanut butter. Cover with the second slice of bread and remove the crusts (so it is easier to eat for young children). Cut into bite-size pieces.

RECOMMENDED FOR AGES 10 MONTHS+

naturally fresh applesauce

8 medium-size apples

Step 1: Preheat the oven to 350°F.

Step 2: Wash and core apples. Place them in a baking dish with ½ inch of water. Cover tightly and bake until tender, 30 minutes for the softer varieties, 45 for harder apples.

Step 3: Strain through a sieve to remove the skin. Use a blender or processor to puree the apple pulp. Store up to one week in the refrigerator or freeze in ice cube trays. Add 3 ounces of pureed soft tofu or ¼ cup cottage cheese to ¼ cup applesauce for a complete lunch.

RECOMMENDED FOR AGES 7 MONTHS +

apples and berries

½ cup peeled, cored, and sliced apples
½ cup washed, hulled, and sliced ripe strawberries (Substitute blueberries for infants under 12 months)

Step 1: Steam the apple slices until tender, about 5 minutes.

Step 2: Combine the strawberries and apples in a food processor, food mill, or blender and process until smooth. Serve at room temperature or chilled. You can add this mixture to baby's morning cereal for variety or add 3 ounces of mashed soft tofu or ¼ cup cottage cheese to make a complete lunch.

RECOMMENDED FOR AGES 12 MONTHS+

apples, plums, and blueberries

1 apple, peeled, cored, and sliced
1 ripe plum, peeled and pitted
¼ cup fresh blueberries, picked over and rinsed, or thawed frozen

Step 1: Steam the sliced apple until tender, about 5 minutes.

Step 2: Combine the apple, plum, and blueberries in a food processor, food mill, or blender and process until smooth. Serve at room temperature or chilled. You can add 3 ounces of pureed soft tofu or ¼ cup cottage cheese, pureed, to make a complete lunch.

RECOMMENDED FOR AGES 7 MONTHS+

apples and apricots

1 apple, peeled, cored, and sliced
1 ripe apricot, peeled and pitted

Step 1: Steam the sliced apple until tender, about 5 minutes.
Step 2: Combine the apple and apricot in a food processor, food mill, or blender and process until smooth. Serve at room temperature or chilled. You can add 3 ounces of pureed soft tofu or ¼ cup cottage cheese, pureed, to make a complete lunch.

RECOMMENDED FOR AGES 7 MONTHS+

stewed dried apricots and tofu

MAKES 2 SERVINGS

1 cup dried apricots
1 ½ cups water
3 ounces soft tofu

Step 1: Soak the apricots in the water for 1 hour.
Step 2: Bring the apricots and water to a boil. Cover and simmer over medium-low heat until tender, 15 to 25 minutes.
Step 3: Let cool. Add the tofu, place in a blender or food processor, and puree.

RECOMMENDED FOR AGES 7 MONTHS+

pears and raspberries

MAKES 2 SERVINGS

2 ripe pears, peeled and cored
1 cup ripe raspberries, gently rinsed and patted dry

Combine all the ingredients in a food processor, food mill, or blender and process until smooth. Serve warm, at room temperature, or chilled. Add 3 ounces of pureed soft tofu or ¼ cup cottage cheese, pureed, to make a complete lunch.

RECOMMENDED FOR AGES 10 MONTHS+

peaches and mango

MAKES 1 TO 2 SERVINGS

1 ripe peach, peeled, pitted, and cut up
1 ripe mango, peeled, pitted, and cut up (papaya may be substituted)

Combine the peach and mango in a food processor, food mill, or blender and puree until smooth. Serve at room temperature or chilled. You can add 3 ounces of pureed soft tofu or ¼ cup cottage cheese, pureed, to make a complete lunch.

RECOMMENDED FOR AGES 7 MONTHS+

mango puree

1 ripe mango, peeled, pitted, and cut into pieces
3 ounces soft tofu or ½ cup cottage cheese

Combine the mango and tofu in a food processor, food mill, or blender and puree. Serve cool or at room temperature.

RECOMMENDED FOR AGES 7 MONTHS+

tropical fruit salad

MAKES 2 SERVINGS

½ avocado, peeled and pitted
½ papaya, peeled and seeded
1 apple, peeled and cored
1 banana, peeled
1 starfruit
4 fresh blueberries, picked over and rinsed
3 ounces soft tofu, pureed (optional)

Slice the fruit, then puree together in a blender, food processor, or food mill. Add the tofu to make a complete lunch. Serve cool or at room temperature.

RECOMMENDED FOR AGES 7 MONTHS+

5

dinner

dinnertime is usually a difficult time for most children and parents. Everyone is tired, and no one really feels like eating. However, we like to have our children at the dinner table with us in the evenings which is not an easy feat. The pace at which we eat is rather rapid, as it is with most families with small children, but having the family together and sharing our day has become important to all of us.

Infants should be fed early so you can concentrate on eating and not feeding the baby. It is easiest to place the baby in a jumper chair or high chair when you eat dinner. We usually offer the baby some of our food or crackers, so that he feels part of the dining process. This way the baby gets to know and understand the dinner-time routine and, once he is old enough, will want to participate in the dinnertime conversation. Dinnertime can be a truly wonderful family experience.

meat

Cook meat until tender but do not overcook it as this will toughen the meat and will make it difficult to puree. Red meat should be cooked to an internal temperature of 150°F, poultry 160°F. Infants and small children should avoid pork, because it tends to be too rich for their digestive systems. Test with a meat thermometer. Remove any fat, skin, bones, or cartilige and cut into small pieces. Puree in a food mill, blender, or food processor. To thin, use ¼ cup milk or formula, cooking juices, or stock for each cup of prepared meat. Cool the pureed meat mixture and freeze it in ice cube trays or small containers. One serving is about ½ cup of meat. Serve within 24 hours.

meat dinner

MAKES 1 SERVING

½ cup cubed cooked meat (lamb, beef, or chicken)
2 tablespoons cooked vegetables (carrots, squash, spinach, peas)
¼ cup cooked rice, potatoes, or noodles
½ cup milk, formula, or broth

Combine all the ingredients and blend in a food processor, food mill, or blender until smooth.

RECOMMENDED FOR AGES 8 MONTHS +

noodles and chicken

1 ½ teaspoons olive oil
¼ pound mushrooms, sliced
1 tablespoon dry milk
2 ¼ teaspoons cornstarch
1 teaspoon low-salt chicken broth
¼ teaspoon minced fresh onion
Pinch of ground nutmeg
1 cup cold water
1 ½ cups broad noodles, cooked according to package instructions and drained
1 ½ cups 2-inch pieces cooked chicken or turkey
1 tablespoon grated Romano cheese

Step 1: Heat the olive oil in a skillet over medium-high heat; add the mushrooms and cook, stirring, until tender.

Step 2: Combine the dry milk, cornstarch, chicken broth, onion, and nutmeg with the cold water in a large saucepan. Cook over medium heat for about 5 minutes until the mixture thickens and bubbles for 1 minute.

Step 3: Arrange the noodles in an 8-cup baking dish. Spread the mushrooms over the noodles; top with the chicken. Pour the sauce over, then sprinkle with the cheese.

Step 4: Bake in a preheated 350°F oven until bubbly, about 30 minutes. Puree in a food processor, food mill, or blender until smooth.

RECOMMENDED FOR AGES 10 MONTHS+

basmati rice and chicken

1 cup basmati rice
2 cups water
1 tablespoon butter or margarine
1 whole chicken breast
¼ cup formula

Step 1: Pick the impurities out of the rice and wash well under cold water, using a fine sieve. Move the rice around with your hands until the water runs clear.

Step 2: Bring the water to a boil, then add the rice and stir with a fork. Reduce the heat to medium-low, cover, and cook for 10 minutes. Remove from the heat and let stand for 10 more minutes. Then add the butter.

Step 3: Meanwhile, bake the chicken in a preheated 350°F oven until tender, about 45 minutes. Remove the skin and bones and shred the meat with your fingers.

Step 4: Place the rice, chicken and formula in a blender, food processor, or food mill and puree until smooth. Serve warm or at room temperature.

RECOMMENDED FOR AGES 8 MONTHS+

sweet potato and chicken dinner

MAKES 1 TO 2 SERVINGS

1 sweet potato, scrubbed
¼ cup cooked white chicken meat, cut into bite-size pieces
1 ripe apricot, peeled and pitted
½ cup cooked brown rice (see page 44)
½ cup formula or other liquid

Step 1: Puncture the skin of the sweet potato with a fork or knife and microwave on high until soft, about 8 minutes. In a conventional oven, bake in a preheated 400°F oven for 45 minutes.

Step 2: When cool enough to handle, scoop out the meat of the sweet potato into a food processor, food mill, or blender. Add the chicken, apricot, brown rice, and ¼ cup of the formula. Blend until smooth. Add more formula until you achieve the desired consistency. Store leftovers in refrigerator for no more than 2 days.

RECOMMENDED FOR AGES 8 MONTHS+

apples and chicken

½ cup apples, peeled, cored, and sliced
½ cup shredded cooked white chicken meat
¼ cup cooked brown rice (see page 44)
½ cup formula

Step 1: Steam the apple slices until tender, about 5 minutes.

Step 2: Combine the apple slices, chicken, rice, and ¼ cup of the formula in a food processor, food mill, or blender and process until smooth. Add more liquid if necessary. Serve warm or at room temperature.

RECOMMENDED FOR AGES 8 MONTHS+

broccoli and chicken dinner

½ cup broccoli florets
¼ cup shredded cooked white chicken meat
¼ cup cooked brown rice (see page 44)
½ cup formula

Step 1: Steam the broccoli until tender, about 5 minutes.

Step 2: Place the broccoli, chicken, rice, and ¼ cup of the formula in a food processor, food mill, or blender and process until smooth. Add more formula if necessary. Serve warm or at room temperature.

RECOMMENDED FOR AGES 8 MONTHS+

vegetable turkey dinner

MAKES 2 SERVINGS

¼ *cup sliced carrots*
½ *apple, peeled, cored, and cut into wedges*
¼ *cup bite-size pieces cooked turkey meat*
½ *cup cooked barley (see page 44)*
½ *cup formula*

Step 1: Place the carrots and apple in a steamer and steam until both are tender, about 5 minutes.

Step 2: Place the carrots, apple, turkey, barley, and ¼ cup of the formula in a food processor, food mill, or blender and process until smooth. Add more formula if needed. Serve warm or at room temperature. Store leftovers in the refrigerator for no more than 2 days.

RECOMMENDED FOR AGES 8 MONTHS+

ham and tropical fruit dinner

¼ *cup peeled, cored, and sliced apple*
½ *cup bite-size pieces cooked ham*
¼ *cup small pieces fresh or canned pineapple*
¼ *cup formula*

Step 1: Steam the apple slices until tender, about 5 minutes.

Step 2: Place the apple slices, ham, pineapple, and 2 tablespoons of the formula in a food processor, food mill, or blender and process until smooth. Add more formula if necessary. Serve warm or at room temperature.

RECOMMENDED FOR AGES 10 MONTHS+

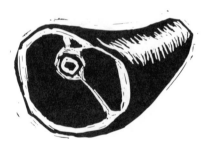

vegetable beef dinner

¼ cup ¼-inch-thick carrot slices
¼ cup bite-size pieces cooked lean beef
¼ cup cooked barley (see page 44)
½ cup formula or other liquid

Step 1: Steam the carrots until tender, about 5 minutes.

Step 2: Combine the carrots, meat, barley and ¼ cup of the formula in a food processor, food mill, or blender and process until smooth. Add more formula liquid if necessary. Serve warm or at room temperature.

RECOMMENDED FOR AGES 8 MONTHS +

spaghetti and beef dinner

¼ cup lean ground beef
½ cup cooked spaghetti (angel hair pasta works well)
1 fresh tomato, peeled, seeded, and cut up

Step 1: Heat a skillet over medium-high heat. Add the ground beef and cook, stirring, until the meat is brown and crumbly.

Step 2: Combine the beef, spaghetti, and tomato in a food processor, food mill, or blender and process until smooth or slightly chunky, depending on what consistency your baby can tolerate. Serve warm or at room temperature.

RECOMMENDED FOR AGES 10 MONTHS+

pasta dinner

½ carrot, cut into ⅛-inch-thick slices
¼ cup cut green beans
½ cup cooked pasta
1 fresh tomato, peeled, seeded, and cut up
¼ cup drained canned chick-peas
¼ cup formula

Step 1: Steam the carrots and green beans together until tender, about 5 minutes.

Step 2: Combine the pasta, tomato, chick-peas, carrot, and green beans in a food processor, food mill, or blender and process until smooth. You may need to add formula to the mixture. Add 2 tablespoons at a time and blend until smooth. Serve warm or at room temperature.

RECOMMENDED FOR AGES 10 MONTHS+

brown rice and lentil dinner

¼ cup ⅛-inch-thick carrot slices
¼ cup ¼-inch-thick peeled apple slices
½ cup cooked brown rice (see page 44)
½ cup cooked lentils
½ cup formula

Step 1: Steam the carrot and apple slices together until both are tender, about 5 minutes.

Step 2: Place the rice, lentils, carrots, apples, and ¼ cup of the formula in a food processor, food mill, or blender and process until smooth. Add more formula until you reach the desired consistency.

RECOMMENDED FOR AGES 8 MONTHS+

potato and green bean dinner

1 potato, peeled and cut into bite-size pieces
¼ cup fresh or frozen cut green beans
¼ cup shredded cheddar cheese
½ cup cooked brown rice (see page 44)
½ cup formula

Step 1: Steam the potato pieces until soft, about 5 minutes.

Step 2: Steam the green beans until soft, 3 to 5 minutes.

Step 3: Place the potato, beans, cheese, rice, and ¼ cup of the formula in a food processor, food mill, or blender and process until smooth. Add more formula until you reach the desired consistency. Serve warm or at room temperature.

RECOMMENDED FOR AGES 8 MONTHS +

summer vegetable dinner

MAKES 4 SERVINGS

¼ cup ½-inch green bean pieces
¼ cup corn kernels
¼ cup ¼-inch-thick zucchini slices
¼ small onion, sliced into ¼-inch wedges
¼ cup ¼-inch-thick carrot slices
¼ cup drained canned chick-peas
½ cup cooked brown rice (see page 44)
¼ cup formula

Step 1: Steam the green beans, corn, zucchini, onions, and carrots together until tender, about 5 minutes.

Step 2: Place the steamed vegetables, chick-peas, rice, and 2 tablespoons of the formula in a food processor, food mill, or blender and process until smooth. Add more formula if you need it. Serve warm or at room temperature.

RECOMMENDED FOR AGES 8 MONTHS+

yogurt potatoes

1 large baking potato
2 tablespoons chopped cooked broccoli
2 tablespoons grated cheddar cheese
2 tablespoons plain yogurt

Step 1: Preheat the oven to 400°F.

Step 2: Prick the potato with a fork in several places, then bake it until tender, about 1 hour.

Step 3: Split the baked potato in half and scoop out the cooked potato. Fill the potato shell with the broccoli, cheese, and potato; bake another 10 minutes. Place the yogurt and baked ingredients in a food processor, food mill, or blender and process until smooth. You may need to add more yogurt for a smooth consistency.

RECOMMENDED FOR AGES 8 MONTHS+

whipped corn potatoes

2 large baking potatoes, peeled and cut into ½-inch pieces
½ to ¾ cup formula or milk
2 tablespoons unsalted butter
Kernels from 2 ears cooked sweet corn

Step 1: Place the potatoes in a large saucepan and cover with water. Cover and bring to a boil over high heat. Lower the heat to medium-low and simmer until tender, about 30 minutes.

Step 2: When the potatoes are done, remove from the heat and drain well. Place in the bowl of a mixer and add the formula and butter. Whip until smooth. Add the corn and puree.

RECOMMENDED FOR AGES 10 MONTHS+. YOU MAY NEED TO STRAIN FOR YOUNGER INFANTS.

pea custard

Chef/Instructor John Jensen, California Culinary Academy

MAKES 4 SERVINGS

1 ½ cups mashed or pureed fresh or frozen (and thawed) peas
2 tablespoons butter or margarine, melted
3 large eggs, well beaten

Step 1: Preheat the oven to 300°F.

Step 2: Combine all the ingredients together well.

Step 3: Pour into lightly greased molds. (Use one large mold or individual serving molds.) Set the molds into a pan filled with water that comes halfway up the sides of the molds.

Step 4: Place the pan in the oven and bake until a paring knife inserted into the center of the mold comes out clean, about 30 minutes.

RECOMMENDED FOR AGES 10 MONTHS+

mashed turnips

Chef/Instructor John Jensen, California Culinary Academy

MAKES 4 SERVINGS

½ pound white or yellow turnips
Pinch of salt
2 tablespoons butter or margarine

Step 1: Wash, peel, and slice the turnips.

Step 2: Place the sliced turnips in a generous amount of boiling water and cook until soft, about 8 to 10 minutes, adding the salt just before the cooking is completed.

Step 3: Drain and mash the turnips in the same pan, then place the pan, uncovered, over low heat for 10 minutes to dry the turnips. Stir the turnips regularly while drying them so they do not scorch or burn. Stir in the butter.

RECOMMENDED FOR AGES 7 MONTHS +

sada's stuffed zucchini

2 zucchini, cut in half lengthwise
3 tablespoons canola or olive oil
1 onion, chopped
1 green bell pepper, seeded and chopped
½ pound lean ground chuck
¼ teaspoon dried oregano

Step 1: Preheat the oven to 350°F.

Step 2: Plunge the zucchini halves into boiling water until tender, 8 to 10 minutes. Drain, scoop out the center pulp to make boats, and retain the pulp. Discard any large seeds.

Step 3: Heat the oil over medium-high heat in a skillet, then add the onions and peppers and cook, stirring, until the onions are golden brown. Add the meat and cook, stirring, until browned, about 10 minutes. Add the oregano and zucchini pulp. Stir well.

Step 4: Place the zucchini boats in two large baking pans. Spoon the hamburger mixture into them. Bake until the tops are brown, 45 to 60 minutes. Puree in a food processor, food mill, or blender until you achieve the desired consistency.

RECOMMENDED FOR AGES 10 MONTHS+

half moons and sunshine

1 ½ tablespoons butter or margarine
½ small onion, grated
1 tablespoon unbleached flour
½ teaspoon dry mustard
1 cup milk
4 ounces cheddar cheese, sliced and cut up
4 ounces elbow macaroni, cooked according to package instructions

Step 1: Melt the butter in a saucepan, then add the onion and cook, stirring, over medium heat until soft. Stir in the flour and mustard; cook, stirring constantly, just until bubbly.

Step 2: Stir in the milk; continue cooking and stirring until the sauce thickens and bubbles, about 3 minutes. Add the cheese, stirring until it melts.

Step 3: Place the drained macaroni in a buttered shallow 8-cup baking dish; pour the cheese sauce over it.

Step 4: Bake in a preheated 350°F oven until bubbly hot, 30 minutes. Puree in a food processor or chop until you have the desired consistency.

RECOMMENDED FOR AGES 10 MONTHS+

6

soups

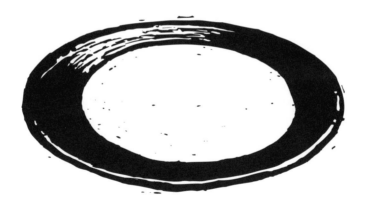

Soups are such a basic kind of dish that they can be offered at lunch and dinner. At lunchtime, you can add a piece of fruit, and you have a well-balanced meal. Children, especially, enjoy soups that are filled with multicolored pastas or alphabet pasta.

Many of these recipes yield adult-size servings which is a perfect way for the entire family to enjoy a meal together.

chicken stock

Executive Chef Suzette Gresham-Tognetti, Ristorante Acquerello

MAKES 4 SERVINGS

One 4 ½-pound chicken
16 cups cold water
1 onion, peeled
2 large carrots, peeled
3 to 4 stalks celery
1 bay leaf
1 clove garlic
½ teaspoon fresh or dried thyme (optional)
¼ bunch fresh parsley sprigs

Step 1: Wash the chicken. Remove any internal parts remaining in the body cavity. Place the chicken in a deep pot and cover with the water.

Step 2: Turn the flame to high. Allow foam to rise to the surface. Skim and discard. Lower the heat to medium and add the remaining ingredients. Maintain the heat at a simmer. Skim the surface occasionally. Allow to cook until the chicken is falling-off-the-bone tender and the liquid seems reduced by about one-third of the original amount, about 30 minutes.

Step 3: Remove from the heat. Gently pour off a portion of the chicken stock while passing through a medium strainer.

Step 4: Transfer the chicken to a serving platter or ovenproof dish. Finish straining the remainder of the broth. Reserve the strained-out vegetables to puree with chicken.

Step 5: Pour the entire quantity of broth through a fine strainer (tea strainer, cheesecloth, etc.) into a container suitable for refrigerator or freezer.

RECOMMENDED FOR AGES 10 MONTHS+

NOTE: *It is easy to produce a quality meal for the entire family, including your infant.*

As a chef, at home the last thing that I want to do is fuss unnecessarily over the stove—so it's one-pot cooking for me! Some of the best foods are the simplest.

This recipe yields chicken stock, but the idea is not to stop there. Try multiplying the yield of your efforts by first serving the whole boiled chicken that evening and either serving the broth with pastina to your infant or perhaps whipping some quick-cooking polenta with it.

The blender or food processor is a key appliance here. Simply by dropping a chunk of chicken and vegetables from the broth into the blender and pureeing, you'll have baby food of the highest quality.

vegetable stock

Chef Tracy Pikhart Ritter

MAKES 6 TO 7 CUPS

1 tablespoon olive oil
2 large onions, chopped
3 large carrots, sliced
2 stalks celery, sliced
1 medium-size potato, peeled and chopped
4 summer squash (zucchini or yellow), chopped
3 tomatoes, peeled, seeded, and chopped
½ cup dried white beans
1 bay leaf
¼ cup parsley stems
2 quarts cold water

Step 1: Heat the oil in a stock pot over medium-high heat; add the onions and cook, stirring, until soft, about 5 minutes. Add the carrots, celery, potato, squash, and tomatoes and cook, stirring, for 15 minutes over medium-low heat. Add the remaining ingredients, bring to a boil, reduce the heat to medium-low, and simmer until the beans are tender, about 1 hour.

Step 2: Strain through cheesecloth. Add pasta and beans to make a complete protein.

RECOMMENDED FOR AGES 8 MONTHS+

savory noodle soup

Chef Martin Yan, Yan Can Cook

MAKES 4 SERVINGS

1 pound egg noodles
5 cups chicken stock (see page 140)
1 teaspoon peeled and minced fresh ginger
½ cup matchstick-size pieces ham
2 cups finely chopped spinach leaves, tough stems removed
4 teaspoons soy sauce

Step 1: Cook the noodles according to the package instructions. Drain, rinse under cold running water, and drain again.

Step 2: In a pot, bring the stock, ginger, and ham to a boil over medium-high heat. Reduce the heat to medium-low and simmer for 2 minutes.

Step 3: Place the noodles in a deep soup bowl. Place the spinach on top of the noodles, sprinkle with soy sauce, and pour the hot broth over all. Puree or chop in a food processor or blender until you reach the desired consistency.

RECOMMENDED FOR AGES 10 MONTHS+

alphabet soup

Executive Chef Reimund Pitz, Epcot Center Foods

1 ½ cups chicken stock (see page 140)
1 ½ cups beef stock
¼ cup diced carrots
¼ cup peeled and diced rutabaga
¼ cup diced celery
¼ cup diced onion
1 cup canned crushed tomatoes
¼ cup frozen peas
¼ cup frozen cut green beans
2 tablespoons cooked pearl barley (see page 44), cooled
¼ cup alphabet noodles, cooked according to package instructions and cooled

Step 1: In a 4-quart soup pot, combine the chicken and beef stock. Bring to a boil and add the carrots, rutabaga, celery, and onion. Reduce the heat to medium and simmer until the vegetables are tender but not mushy, about 15 minutes.

Step 2: Add the tomatoes, peas, and green beans. Simmer an additional 5 minutes, then add the pearl barley and alphabet noodles. Heat only long enough to warm all the ingredients. Puree in a food processor or blender. Serve immediately.

RECOMMENDED FOR AGES 8 MONTHS+

riso e patate (rice and potato soup)

Chef/Owner Lidia Bastianich, Felidia Ristorante

MAKES 4 SERVINGS

3 tablespoons olive oil
2 potatoes, peeled and cut into ¼-inch dice
2 carrots, shredded
2 stalks celery, halved
2 teaspoons tomato paste
10 cups chicken stock (see page 140)
2 bay leaves
1 cup long-grain rice

Step 1: In a deep pot or large saucepan, heat the olive oil over medium-high heat. Add the potatoes and cook, turning occasionally, until browned, about 5 minutes. Add the carrots and celery, and cook 2 to 3 minutes over medium heat, stirring with a wooden spoon. Add the tomato paste, stock, and bay leaves. Cover the pot and simmer 40 minutes over medium-low heat.

Step 2: Add the rice and cook until it is tender, 12 minutes longer. Remove the celery and bay leaves. Puree or chop in a food processor or blender. Serve warm or at room temperature.

RECOMMENDED FOR AGES 8 MONTHS+

nicolai's borscht

2 carrots, sliced
1 ½ cups peeled and shredded beets
1 turnip, peeled and diced
1 medium-size onion, sliced
1 cup water
2 tablespoons cider vinegar
6 cups beef stock
2 cups diced cooked beef
½ small cabbage, shredded

Step 1: Combine the carrots, beets, turnip, onion, water, and vinegar in a 2- or 3-quart saucepan. Bring to a boil, then reduce the heat to medium, cover, and simmer 20 minutes. Add the stock, beef, and cabbage and simmer until all the vegetables are tender, 10 to 15 minutes.

Step 2: Puree in a food processor or blender and serve warm or at room temperature.

RECOMMENDED FOR AGES 8 MONTHS +

potato soup

5 medium-size leeks
2 tablespoons butter or margarine
1 small onion, finely chopped
3 medium-size potatoes, peeled and cut into ½-inch dice
4 cups boiling water
3 cups milk

Step 1: Cut off root ends and tops of the leeks. Clean, drain, and slice them about ¼ inch thick.

Step 2: In a 3- to 4-quart saucepan over medium heat, melt the butter. Add the leeks and onion and cook, stirring often, until soft but not browned. Mix in the potatoes and boiling water. Bring to a boil, cover, reduce the heat slightly, and cook until the potatoes are very tender, 25 to 30 minutes.

Step 3: Puree the mixture in two or three batches in a blender or food processor until smooth. Return to the cooking pan and stir in the milk. Stir over medium heat until steaming hot. Cover and refrigerate 3 to 5 hours or overnight.

RECOMMENDED FOR AGES 10 MONTHS+

sweet potato soup

Executive Chef Bernd W. Liebergesell, the Westin St. Francis Hotel

MAKES 4 SERVINGS

2 tablespoons unsalted butter or margarine
½ cup finely chopped onion
1 cup finely chopped leeks (white part only and well washed)
1 large clove garlic, minced
3 large carrots, thinly sliced
1 bay leaf
1 ½ pounds large sweet potatoes, peeled and cut into ¼-inch cubes
¾ pound russet potatoes, cut into ¼-inch cubes
6 cups chicken stock (see page 140)
2 cups water

Step 1: In a large stock pot, melt the butter over medium heat, then add the onions, leeks, garlic, carrots and bay leaf and cook, stirring, until softened, about 8 to 10 minutes.

Step 2: Add the potatoes, chicken stock, and water and simmer until everything is soft, 25 to 30 minutes. Discard the bay leaf.

Step 3: In a blender or food processor, puree the soup in small batches until very smooth.

RECOMMENDED FOR AGES 8 MONTHS+

carrot soup

Executive Chef Patrizio Sacchetto, Umberto's

MAKES 4 SERVINGS

¼ cup (½ stick) butter or margarine
2 yellow onions, finely chopped
1 ¼ pounds carrots, finely diced
2 ½ cups chicken stock (see page 140)
3 tablespoons medium- or long-grain rice
¾ to 1 cup milk

Step 1: In a medium-size heavy saucepan, melt 2 tablespoons of the butter. Add the onions and carrots and cook over low heat about 10 minutes.

Step 2: Add the stock and rice and bring to a boil. Reduce the heat to low, cover, and cook until the carrots and rice are very tender, about 30 minutes.

Step 3: Transfer the carrots, rice, and the cooking juices to a blender or food processor and puree until smooth.

Step 4: Return to the saucepan and simmer, uncovered, over low heat, stirring often, for 5 minutes. Add ¾ cup of the milk and bring the soup to a boil. If the soup is too thick, stir in the remaining milk. Taste for seasoning. Soup can be kept, covered, up to two days in the refrigerator. If necessary, reheat the soup over medium-low heat, stirring.

Step 5: Stir in the remaining 2 tablespoons of butter. Puree in a food processor to remove any lumps or until smooth. Serve warm or at room temperature.

RECOMMENDED FOR AGES 10 MONTHS+

minestra di funghi selvatici (wild mushroom soup)

Chef/Owner Lidia Bastianich, Felidia Ristorante

MAKES 6 SERVINGS

8 pieces (⅔ ounce) dried porcini mushrooms
1 ½ cups warm water
5 tablespoons olive oil
1 medium-size onion, chopped
2 medium-size potatoes, peeled and cut into ¼-inch cubes
2 medium-size carrots, sliced
1 large shallot, chopped
2 ½ quarts chicken stock (see page 140)

Step 1: Soak the mushrooms in the water until softened, about 20 minutes. Drain, reserving all but the last 2 teaspoons of the steeping liquid (to avoid unwanted sediments). Remove and rinse the softened porcini.

Step 2: In a 5-quart pot, heat the olive oil over medium heat, then add the onion and cook, stirring, until translucent. Add the potatoes, carrots, and shallot and cook 2 minutes, stirring occasionally. Add the stock, drained porcini, and reserved soaking liquid, and bring to a boil. Reduce the heat and keep at a low boil until the vegetables are tender, about 10 minutes. Puree in a food processor or blender until smooth.

RECOMMENDED FOR AGES 8 MONTHS+

garden vegetable soup

2 medium-size potatoes, cut into ½-inch cubes
2 medium-size carrots, cut into ¼-inch slices
1 cup diced string beans
1 medium-size onion, diced
2 medium-size summer squash, cut into ¼-inch slices
2 large stalks celery, cut into ¼-inch slices
3 medium-size tomatoes, peeled, seeded, and cut into small pieces
¼ large green bell pepper, seeded and cut into ¼-inch strips
½ teaspoon minced garlic
½ cup pearl barley, brown rice, or whole-wheat pasta

Step 1: Place the vegetables in a large saucepan and add water to cover. Bring to a boil and add the garlic. Simmer over medium heat until the vegetables are nearly tender, about 15 minutes.

Step 2: Add the barley and continue to cook until tender. Puree in a food processor or blender. Serve warm.

RECOMMENDED FOR AGES 8 MONTHS+

minestrone

MAKES 8 TO 10 SERVINGS

1 cup dried white beans
11 cups water
2 tablespoons olive oil
2 ⅓ to 3 pounds ¾- to 1-inch-thick beef shanks
2 large onions, slivered
2 large carrots, chopped
2 stalks celery, thinly sliced
2 cloves garlic, minced or pressed
½ cup chopped fresh parsley
1 ham hock
One 28-ounce can whole tomatoes, coarsely chopped
1 medium-size turnip, peeled and diced
2 cups chopped Swiss chard leaves, tough stems removed
½ cup fresh or frozen peas
1 ½ cups hot cooked rice
2 cups shredded cabbage

Step 1: Place the beans in a large bowl and add 3 cups of the water. Cover and let stand for at least 8 hours; drain, discarding the soaking liquid. (Or, to shorten the soaking period, place the beans in a 2- to 3-quart pot with 4 cups water, bring to a boil and boil briskly, uncovered, for 2 minutes. Remove from the heat, cover, and let stand for 1 hour. Drain, discarding the soaking liquid.)

THE WELL-FED BABY
152

Step 2: In a 7- to 8-quart kettle, heat the olive oil over medium heat. Add the beef shanks and brown on all sides. As you turn the shanks to brown the last side, add the onions; cook, stirring occasionally, until the onions are limp.

Step 3: Add the carrots, celery, garlic, parsley, ham hock, tomatoes along with their liquid, soaked beans, and the remaining 8 cups of water. Bring to a boil, cover, reduce the heat to medium, and simmer until the meat and beans are tender, 3 ½ to 4 hours. Skim and discard any surface fat.

Step 4: Remove the beef shanks and ham hock with a slotted spoon. When cool enough to handle, discard the bones and skin. Return the beef and ham in large chunks to the soup.

Step 5: Add the turnip and simmer over medium heat, uncovered, for 10 minutes. Mix in the chard and peas and cook for 3 minutes more. Blend in the rice and cabbage and cook, stirring occasionally, just until the cabbage is wilted and bright green, 3 to 5 minutes. Puree in a food processor or blender.

RECOMMENDED FOR AGES 10 MONTHS+

noodles and bean soup

MAKES 12 SERVINGS

1 pound dried pinto beans
½ cup olive oil
1 ½ cups chopped onions
3 tablespoons minced garlic
3 bay leaves
One 6-ounce can tomato paste
One 28-ounce can tomato puree
10 cups water
1 cup favorite small pasta noodles

Step 1: Cover the beans with cold water to cover and soak overnight.

Step 2: Heat the olive oil in a large soup pot. Add the onions, garlic, and bay leaves and cook over low heat, stirring occasionally, until the onions and garlic are soft and translucent, 10 to 15 minutes.

Step 3: Add the tomato paste and puree and cook another 5 mintues. Stir in the water, cover partially, and cook over medium heat for 20 minutes.

Step 4: Drain the beans and add them to the kettle. Reduce the heat to medium-low, cover, and simmer until the beans are tender, about 1 ½ hours.

Step 5: Add the pasta and continue to simmer until the pasta is tender, another 10 minutes. Puree or chop in a food processor or blender to the desired consistency.

RECOMMENDED FOR AGES 10 MONTHS +

beef and bean soup

2 tablespoons butter or margarine
1 pound lean steak, cut into 1/4-inch pieces
One 28-ounce can whole tomatoes, drained
1 cup beef stock
1 cup water
1/2 cup barley
1/4 cup chopped onion
One 10-ounce package frozen lima beans
One 10-ounce package frozen Italian beans
One 8-ounce can butter beans, drained

Step 1: Melt the butter in a skillet over medium-high heat. Add the steak and cook, stirring, until browned on all sides.

Step 2: Stir in the tomatoes, stock, water, barley, and onion. Bring to a boil, reduce the heat to medium, and let simmer 50 minutes.

Step 3: Stir in the lima beans and Italian beans. Bring to a boil, reduce the heat to medium, cover, and simmer 10 minutes.

Step 4: Stir in the butter beans. Cover and simmer 10 minutes. Puree the soup in a food processor or blender.

RECOMMENDED FOR AGES 8 MONTHS+

navy bean soup

1 cup dried navy beans
9 cups water
1 ½ teaspoons olive oil
1 cup chopped onion
2 cloves garlic, crushed
2 medium-size carrots, chopped
2 stalks celery, chopped

Step 1: Rinse the beans, then soak them in 3 cups of the water for a minimum of 3 hours or overnight. Drain, then place in a large, heavy pot.

Step 2: Add the remaining water, bring to a boil, lower the heat to medium, and simmer, covered, until tender, about 1 hour. (If you like, after 30 minutes, replace the cooking water with an equal amount of fresh water. This helps reduce the gassy effect of the beans.)

Step 3: Heat the olive oil in a skillet over medium heat. Add the onion and garlic and cook, stirring, until soft. When the beans are cooked or nearly cooked, add this mixture to them along with the carrots and celery. Simmer another 10 minutes. Puree in a food processor or blender and serve warm or at room temperature.

RECOMMENDED FOR AGES 8 MONTHS +

quick and delicious split pea soup

1 cup dried split peas, rinsed and picked over
3 ¼ cups water
1 cup chopped onion
1 cup chopped celery
1 ¼ cups sliced carrots

Step 1: Place the peas, water, onion, and celery in a medium-size pot, bring just to a boil, then reduce the heat to low, cover, and simmer until the peas are tender, about 40 minutes.

Step 2: Put the soup in a food processor or blender and puree until smooth. Then add the sliced carrots and blend briefly, just enough to have bits of carrot in the soup (unless you want it totally smooth). Return the soup to the pot and cook for another 10 minutes. Serve warm or at room temperature.

RECOMMENDED FOR AGES 8 MONTHS+

lentil chicken soup

2 tablespoons butter or margarine
1 small onion, thinly slivered
¼ cup finely chopped celery
¼ cup finely chopped fresh parsley
1 medium-size carrot, shredded
½ cup dried lentils, rinsed and drained
3 cups chicken stock (see page 140)

Step 1: In a 2- to 3-quart saucepan over medium heat, melt the butter. Add the onion, celery, parsley, and carrot and cook, stirring often, until the vegetables are soft but not browned, about 5 to 8 minutes. Add the lentils and stock.

Step 2: Bring the soup to a boil, cover, and reduce the heat to medium. Stirring occasionally so the lentils don't stick to the bottom, simmer until the lentils are tender, 25 to 30 minutes.

Step 3: Puree in a food processor or blender and serve warm or at room temperature.

RECOMMENDED FOR AGES 8 MONTHS+

7

snacks and desserts

We feel that nutritious desserts should be a part of the regular meal plan, rather than be served at the end of the meal as a "big treat." Moderation is the key to healthy eating, which includes eating dessert. The following dessert recipes yield child-size portions and offer variety using a combination of healthful ingredients.

A small child who cannot eat much at mealtime may need to snack. Snacks should not be junk food but should contribute to your baby's nutrition. Snacks need not be fancy but should be nutritious and delicious.

Children should be served their snack, be allowed to eat it, and then be finished eating until the next meal. If they are allowed to eat from the cupboards and refrigerator at will, they may turn the day into one continuous snack period. Meals can have little meaning and many medical and weight problems may result. Remember that your child will want the same foods that you eat. Choose snacks that are good for your health. You can make healthy snacks from foods that you have around the house.

Some good snacks are:

babies 6 to 8 months

Mashed soft-cooked vegetables
Cottage cheese
Graham or unsalted soda crackers

Ripe banana
Toast strips
Plain bread sticks
Fruit juice, fruit shake, or yogurt drink
Fruit popsicles
Zwieback
Whole bagel

babies 9 to 12 months

Soft-cooked vegetables
Peaches, apples, pears, apricots, papayas, bananas, raw or canned, peeled, pitted, and cut into small pieces
Soft cheese
Well-cooked hamburger, broken into small pieces
Egg yolk
Strips of tender beef or chicken, cut into small pieces
Cottage cheese
Water-packed canned tuna
Toast
Yogurt
Cubes of cooked potato
Toasted whole-grain waffle, cut into small pieces
Dry unsweetened cereal (like Cheerios) with milk
Graham crackers, oatmeal cookies
Fruit juice

Cheese cubes
Quick breads such as banana or pumpkin, cut into small pieces
Pretzels
Rice cakes
Banana sandwich
Melted cheese on toast

perfect peanut butter

MAKES 2 CUPS

One 16-ounce bag unsalted peanuts
2 tablespoons peanut oil

Shell the peanuts, also removing their skins, and place them in a blender or food processor. Add the oil and process until smooth and creamy. Add more oil if necessary.

RECOMMENDED FOR AGES 10 MONTHS+

golden cheese puffs

MAKES 24

1 cup grated cheddar cheese
1 cup unbleached flour
¼ cup vegetable oil

Step 1: Stir all the ingredients together, add just enough water to moisten the mixture, and refrigerate about 15 minutes.

Step 2: Roll the dough into small balls and place them on a greased cookie sheet. Bake 12 minutes in a preheated 400°F oven. Cut into bite-size pieces and store in a clean airtight container. They will keep refrigerated for up to 1 week.

RECOMMENDED FOR AGES 10 MONTHS+

pretzel crisps

1 cup warm water
1 envelope active yeast
1 tablespoon sugar
2 ½ cups unbleached flour
1 large egg yolk, beaten

Step 1: Mix the water, yeast, and sugar together and set aside for 15 minutes. Add the flour and knead 5 minutes.

Step 2: Cut into small pieces and roll the pieces into ropes. Twist the ropes into the traditional pretzel shapes. Brush the tops with the beaten egg.

Step 3: Bake in a preheated 425°F oven until golden brown, 15 to 20 minutes. Offer stale or frozen.

Note: For Quick and Easy Pretzels, make this recipe with thawed store-bought frozen bread dough.

RECOMMENDED FOR AGES 10 MONTHS+

yogurt fruit crunch

MAKES 4 SERVINGS

2 cups plain yogurt
1 cup granola cereal
1 cup pureed fruit

Spoon layers of the yogurt, cereal, and fruit into four individual bowls.

RECOMMENDED FOR AGES 10 MONTHS+

yum's yogurt

MAKES 2 SERVINGS

1 cup fruit, peeled, seeded, and diced
¼ cup frozen apple juice concentrate
1 cup plain yogurt

Process all the ingredients together in a food processor or blender until smooth.

RECOMMENDED FOR AGES 7 MONTHS+

mixed berries and yogurt mold

Executive Chef Rick Pestana, Epcot Center Foods

MAKES 2 SERVINGS

1 cup natural strawberry yogurt
1 cup pureed mixed fresh blueberries and raspberries
1 teaspoon unflavored gelatin
2 tablespoons boiling water

Step 1: Coat the inside rim of two 3- or 3 ½-inch cookie cutters with vegetable oil. Set the cookie cutters in the middle of a dinner plate and set in the refrigerator to cool.

Step 2: Combine the yogurt and berries in a bowl. Dissolve the gelatin in the boiling water, then add to the yogurt and berries mixture; mix well. Fill the cookie cutters with the yogurt mixture and place in the refrigerator to set, 35 to 40 minutes. When ready to serve, pull the cookie cutters from the plate.

RECOMMENDED FOR AGES 10 MONTHS+

summer berry gelatin

Jennifer Hoolhorst, The American Institute of Wine and Food

MAKES 6 SERVINGS

1 envelope unflavored gelatin
2 cups strawberry nectar (available in the juice section of the supermarket)
1 ½ cups fresh raspberries, blackberries, or boysenberries, pureed

Step 1: Mix the gelatin with ½ cup of the juice. Heat the remaining juice in a saucepan just until it reaches a boil. Combine the hot juice and gelatin mixture. Chill the mixture until it thickens to the consistency of unbeaten egg whites.

Step 2: Meanwhile, place ¼ cup of the pureed berries into each of six dessert dishes. When the gelatin is thickened, give it a stir (the juice may have separated out) and pour it over the pureed berries. Chill until firm.

RECOMMENDED FOR AGES 10 MONTHS+

baked banana pudding

Chef Bernd W. Liebergesell, the Westin St. Francis Hotel

MAKES 4 SERVINGS

⅓ *cup sugar*
2 tablespoons unbleached flour
2 large eggs
⅔ *cup milk*
2 teaspoons pure vanilla extract
1 large banana, peeled and cut into ¼-inch slices

Step 1: In a blender, mix together the sugar, flour, eggs, milk, and vanilla. Blend until smooth.

Step 2: Butter a small casserole dish and layer the sliced bananas in it. Pour the blended pudding mixture over the bananas and bake in a preheated 400°F oven until the mixture is firm, 20 to 25 minutes.

RECOMMENDED FOR AGES 10 MONTHS+

rice pudding

2 cups cooked brown rice (see page 44)
2 cups milk
½ cup dry milk
¼ cup firmly packed brown sugar
1 tablespoon margarine, melted
2 large eggs, beaten
½ teaspoon pure vanilla extract
Plain bread crumbs or wheat germ

Step 1: Preheat the oven to 350°F.

Step 2: Mix all the ingredients together except the bread crumbs.

Step 3: Grease a 1-quart ovenproof casserole dish and sprinkle the bottom with the bread crumbs. Pour in the pudding mixture and sprinkle more crumbs on top. Bake until a knife inserted in the center comes out clean, about 20 minutes. Serve cold.

RECOMMENDED FOR AGES 8 MONTHS+

fruit custard

MAKES 2 SERVINGS

¼ *cup fruit puree (banana, peach, pear)*
1 egg yolk, beaten
¼ *cup milk*

Step 1: Preheat the oven to 350°F.

Step 2: Blend all the ingredients together. Pour into two custard cups and place in a pan of water so that the water comes ½ inch up the sides of the custard cups.

Step 3: Bake until a knife comes out clean when inserted into the center of the custard, about 30 minutes. This will keep in the refrigerator up to 3 days.

RECOMMENDED FOR AGES 10 MONTHS+

tofu custard

3 large eggs
1 cup firm tofu
2 tablespoons rice malt sweetener (located in the specialty food section of the
    supermarket)
1 cup milk
1 teaspoon pure vanilla extract
½ teaspoon ground cinnamon

Step 1: Preheat the oven to 350°F. Lightly butter a 1 ½-quart casserole dish.

Step 2: Beat the eggs in a medium-size bowl.

Step 3: In a blender or food processor, process the tofu, sweetener, milk, vanilla, and cinnamon together until smooth. Pour the blended mixture into the bowl with the beaten eggs and stir, mixing well.

Step 4: Pour the custard mixture into the buttered casserole dish. Bake until the top is light brown or when a knife inserted in the middle comes out clean, about 1 hour.

RECOMMENDED FOR AGES 8 MONTHS+

tofutti

MAKES 1 SERVING

3 ounces soft tofu
¼ banana, peeled
¼ peach, peeled and pitted

Step 1: Puree all the ingredients in a food processor or blender.
Step 2: Pour into small plastic containers and freeze until semisoft, like ice cream.

RECOMMENDED FOR AGES 8 MONTHS+

banana ice cream

Executive Chef Amy Ferguson-Ota, the Ritz Carlton Mauna Lai

MAKES 4 SERVINGS

6 very ripe bananas

Step 1: Peel the bananas and freeze until firm.
Step 2: You will need a strong juicer or extractor. Process the bananas as you would any juice. They become a creamy, frozen banana icelike dessert.

RECOMMENDED FOR AGES 8 MONTHS+

frozen fruit pops

One 1-pound bag frozen fruit, thawed
¾ cup juice of choice (apple, pear, cherry)

Step 1: Pour the fruit and juice into blender or food processor and blend until the fruit and juice look like smooth, thick soup.

Step 2: Fill 5-ounce paper cups with the fruit mixture to ¼ inch below the top and place in the freezer.

Step 3: After 1 hour, when the fruit mixture should be partially frozen, put a plastic or wooden stick into the center of each cup. Return the cups to the freezer. In about 3 hours, the fruit mixture should be completely frozen.

Step 4: Take a cup out and warm it between your hands until the popsicle can be pulled out of the cup by the handle.

RECOMMENDED FOR AGES 8 MONTHS+

tips for eating out with the well-fed baby

after a busy day, cooking is not the first item on your agenda. Here are a few suggestions for taking your family out for dinner.

Fast-food restaurants cater specifically to children, because they offer not only food but place mats to color, monkey bars, swings, slides, and rides that will keep them occupied while you finish eating. Many offer fresh vegetable or salad bars.

Ethnic dining can be a treat for children, because many ethnic restaurants are especially tolerant of children and also offer wonderful amenities. Many ethnic foods such as po-po platters, quesadillas, pot stickers, tempura, and noodle dishes really appeal to the young diner.

Talk to the chef, manager, or server. Usually they can arrange to have the sauce left off a particular dish or served on the side and reduce or eliminate hot spices.

Dining in off-peak hours or early in the evening is usually your best bet, as then the young diner may receive special attention from the staff. Young diners are usually at their best in the early evening.

Refrain from ordering multicourse meals, or, if you do, make sure that the waiter brings the children's entrées when the first course is served to the adults.

Be sure to ask if there are high chairs or booster seats. Parents should ask if they can bring a stroller into a restaurant.

Parents should set realistic goals for their children's behavior. Lay down a few ground rules before you get to the restaurant.

Tuck suction-cup toys, rattles, and pacifiers into a pocket or purse, and consider packing a snack.

If the child does act up, escort the child from the table out of the dining room or restaurant. There is nothing worse than having a child pitch a fit in a restaurant. Remember, other diners may have paid for a sitter to stay home with their children. Remain with the upset child in the restroom, lounge area, or outside until he gets his act together.

You can entertain your child with a bowl of chipped ice.

Ask for a package of crackers right away.

Grilled cheese and baked potatoes are popular with children.

If you order soup, you can spoon out the vegetables and meat for the baby.

Bring a garlic press with you. It can mince up food very nicely.

Tell the staff that you want to order right away.

Feed a snack or small meal to the child prior to going out, because sometimes it can be a long wait before being served.

Always be prepared.

Leave a fair tip, 15 to 20 percent. The staff will welcome you back!

the contributing chefs

the following chefs contributed their time and recipes to the compilation of this cookbook. However, some of the recipes were not included, but we would like to thank them for their time and effort by mentioning them and their place of business.

Chef/Owner Lidia Bastianich
Felidia Ristorante
243 East 58th Street
New York, NY 10022

Phyllis Bologna, Executive Chef for National Accounts Development
General Foods USA Foodservice Division
250 North Street EG3
White Plains, NY 10625

Chef/Author Flo Braker
1441 Edgewood Drive
Palo Alto, CA 94301

Chef Dennis Clews CEC (Certified Executive Chef)
Stanford Park Hotel
100 El Camino Real
Menlo Park, CA 94025

Chef/Owner Bert Cutino
Executive Chef Karl Ilie Staub
Sardine Factory
701 Wave Street
Monterey, CA 93940

Executive Chef Roger Dikon
Makena Resort
5400 Makena Alanui
Kihei, Hawaii 96753

Chef/Author Dean Fearing
The Mansion on Turtle Creek
2821 Turtle Creek Boulevard
Dallas, TX 75219

Executive Chef Amy Ferguson-Ota
The Ritz Carlton Mauna Lai
One North Kaniku Drive
Kohala Coast, Big Island of Hawaii 96743

Chef/Instructor/Author Bo Friberg
California Culinary Academy
625 Polk Street
San Francisco, CA 94102

Corporate Executive Chef Roberto Gerometta
Nestlé Brands Foodservice Company
800 North Brand Boulevard
Glendale, CA 91203

Chef/Director of Programs Jennifer Hoolhorst
The American Institute of Wine and Food
1550 Bryant Street, Suite 700
San Francisco, CA 94103

Chef/Instructor John T. Jensen
California Culinary Academy
625 Polk Street
San Francisco, CA 94102

Chef/Owner Hubert Keller
Fleur De Lys
777 Sutter Street
San Francisco, CA 94109

President of the American Culinary Federation/Chef Keith Keogh
Epcot Center Foods
Orlando, FL 32819

Chef/Instructor Lars Kronmark
California Culinary Academy
625 Polk Street
San Francisco, CA 94102

Executive Chef Bernd W. Liebergesell
The Westin St. Francis Hotel
335 Powell Street
San Francisco, CA 94102

Chef/Owner Emil Moser
Emiles
545 South Second Street
San Jose, CA 95112

Chef/Instructor Mial Parker
California Culinary Academy
625 Polk Street
San Francisco, CA 94102

Chef/Owner Cindy Pawlcyn
Mustards Grill/Fog City Diner
180 Harbor Drive, Suite 100
Sausalito, CA 94965

Executive Chef Rick Pestana
Epcot Center Foods
Orlando, FL 32819

Executive Chef Reimund Pitz
Epcot Center Foods
Orlando, FL 32819

Chef/Author Tracy Pikhart Ritter
Stamina Cuisine
San Diego, CA 92660

Executive Chef Patrizio Sacchetto
Umberto's
141 Steuart Street
San Francisco, CA 94105

Charles Saunders, Executive Chef/Owner, Eastside Oyster Bar & Grill
133 East Napa Street
Sonoma, CA 95476

Chef Nadar Sharkes
Chef Instructor Diablo Valley College
Diablo, CA 94506

Suzette Gresham-Tognetti, Executive Chef/Owner, Ristorante Acquerello
1722 Sacramento
San Francisco, CA 94109

Chef Hans Wiegand
The Claremont Resort and Tennis Club
Ashby and Domingo Avenues
Oakland, CA 94623

Chef Instructor/Author Kenneth C. Wolfe
P.O. Box 456
Lafayette, CA 94549

Chef/Author/TV Personality Martin Yan
Yan Can Cook
1064 G Shell Boulevard
Foster City, CA 94404

index

a

acorn squash and brown rice, 94
alphabet soup, 144
apple(s):
    and apricots, 110
    and berries, 108
    carrot puree, 90
    carrots and beets with, 88
    and chicken, 120
    -date yogurt breakfast, 51
    -orange muffins, 79
    plums, and blueberries, 109
    and sweet potato puree, 97
applesauce:
    naturally fresh, 107
    and pear, chunky, 52
apricots:
    and apples, 110
    stewed dried, and tofu, 110

b

bagels, Chef Rachel's, 74-75
banana(s):
    and barley, 54
    bread sticks, 76
    ice cream, 173
    monkey sandwich, 106
    peach oatmeal, 53

banana(s) *(cont.)*
    plums, and rice, 53
    pudding, baked, 169
barley:
    and banana, 54
    and beets, 87
    and chick-pea puree, 92
basmati rice and chicken, 118
Bastianich, Lidia, 80, 145, 150
bean(s), 84
    and beef soup, 155
    green, and potato dinner, 128
    navy, soup, 156
    and noodle soup, 154
    red, and ham, Bibby's, 98
    refried, 100
    vegetarian chili, 99
beef:
    and bean soup, 155
    and spaghetti dinner, 125
    vegetable dinner, 124
beets:
    and barley, 87
    and carrots with apple, 88
berry(ies):
    and apples, 108

    mixed, and yogurt mold, 167
    summer, gelatin, 168
Bibby's red beans and ham, 98
biscuits:
    oatmeal shortbread, 69
    sturdy teething, 73
blueberry(ies):
    apples, and plums, 109
    breakfast popovers, 68
    yogurt breakfast, 50
Bologna, Phyllis, 69
borscht, Nicolai's, 146
breads, 65-80
breakfast recipes, 41-63
broccoli and chicken dinner, 121
Bronwyn's favorite cereal, 59
brown rice:
    and acorn squash, baked, 94
    and baby carrots, 91
    hippie burger, 101
    and lentil dinner, 127
    and peas, 96
bunny muffins, 77
butternut squash and corn, 93

c

carrot(s):
  apple puree, 90
  baby, and brown rice, 91
  and beets with apple, 88
  puree with mint, 89
  soup, 149
cereal, Bronwyn's favorite, 59
cheese puffs, golden, 164
cherry tapioca, 57
chicken:
  and apples, 120
  and basmati rice, 118
  and broccoli dinner, 121
  california, 104
  lentil soup, 158
  and noodles, 117
  stock, 140-141
  and sweet potato dinner, 119
  and wehoni rice, 105
chick-pea puree and barley, 92
chili beans, vegetarian, 99
contributing chefs, 177-182
corn:
  and butternut squash, 93
  whipped potatoes, 131

cottage cheese fruit, 49
couscous and eggplant, 95
custard:
  fruit, 171
  pea, 132
  tofu, 172
Cutino, Bert, 68

d

date-apple yogurt breakfast, 51
desserts and snacks, 161-174
dietary allowances (RDA), 14-16
dinner recipes, 113-135

e

eating guides, 36-39
eating out with baby, 175-176
eggplant and couscous, 95
egg(s):
  frittata, 61
  and grits, 60
  one-eyed pete, 62

egg(s) *(cont.)*
 yolk, breakfast, 46

f

farina, fruity, 56
feeding guides, 13, 17-39
Ferguson-Ota, Amy, 173
Friberg, Bo, 70
frittata, 61
fruit(s), 27-28
 chunky, 47
 compote, 48
 cooked, 47
 cottage cheese, 49
 custard, 171
 frozen pops, 174
 juice, 27
 raw, 46
 tropical, and ham dinner, 123
 tropical salad, 112
 tropical treat, 49
 yogurt crunch, 166
 see also specific fruits
fruity farina, 56

g

graham crackers, 75
grains, preparing, 44, 45
Gresham-Tognetti, Suzette, 98, 140
grits and eggs, 60

h

half moons and sunshine, 135
ham:
 and red beans, Bibby's, 98
 tropical fruit dinner, 123
hippie burger, 101
honey, 11
Hoolhorst, Jennifer, 168

i

ice cream, banana, 173

j

Jensen, John, 57, 132, 133

l

legumes, 84
lentil(s), 84
    and brown rice dinner, 127
    chicken soup, 158
    hippie burger, 101
Liebergesell, Bernd W., 148, 169
lunch recipes, 81-112

m

mango:
    and peaches, 111
    puree, 112
meat:
    cooking, 115-116
    dinner, 116
millet and peaches, 55
minestra di funghi selvatici, 150
minestrone, 152-153
monkey sandwich, 106
muffins:
    apple-orange, 79
    bunny, 77
    pumpkin, 78

n

Nicolai's borscht, 146
noodle(s):
    and bean soup, 154
    and chicken, 117
    savory soup, 143

o

oatmeal:
    peach banana, 53
    shortbread biscuits, 69
one-eyed pete, 62
orange-apple muffins, 79

p

Parker, Mial, 59
pasta dinner, 126
peach(es):
    banana oatmeal, 53
    and mango, 111
    and millet, 55
peanut butter, perfect, 163

pear(s):
    and applesauce, chunky, 52
    and raspberries, 111
pea(s), 84
    and brown rice, 96
    custard, 132
    split, soup, 157
Pestana, Rick, 167
Pitz, Reimund, 144
plums:
    apples, and blueberries, 109
    bananas, and rice, 53
    and yogurt, 50
polenta, basic, 80
popovers, blueberry, 68
potato(es):
    and green bean dinner, 128
    and rice soup, 145
    soup, 147
    starch solution, 72
    whipped corn, 131
    yogurt, 130
pretzel crisps, 165
pudding:
    baked banana, 169
    rice, 170

pumpkin muffins, 78

r

raspberries and pears, 111
refried beans, 100
rice:
    breakfast, 58
    congee, 103
    plums, and bananas, 53
    pudding, 170
riso e patate, 145
Ritter, Tracy Pikhart, 142

s

Sacchetto, Patrizio, 149
Sada's stuffed zucchini, 134
servings, recommended, 35-39
shortbread oatmeal biscuits, 69
snacks, 161-174
soups, 137-158
spaghetti and beef dinner, 125
squash:
    acorn, and brown rice, 94

squash (*cont.*)
    butternut, and corn, 93
    Sada's stuffed zucchini, 134
straining food, 14
sweet potato:
    and apple puree, 97
    and chicken dinner, 119
    soup, 148

t

tabbouleh salad, 102
tapioca, cherry, 57
teeth, 11-12, 33-34
teething biscuits, sturdy, 73
teething foods, 23-24
tofu, 26
    custard, 172
    scrambled, 63
    and stewed dried apricots, 110
tofutti, 173
tropical treat, 49
turkey vegetable dinner, 122
turnips, mashed, 133

v

vegetable(s), 26
    beef dinner, 124
    cooked, 85
    frittata, 61
    garden, soup, 151
    steamed, 86
    stock, 142
    summer, dinner, 129
    turkey dinner, 122
    see also specific vegetables
vegetarian chili beans, 99

w

wehoni rice and chicken, 105
wild mushroom soup, 150
Wolfe, Kenneth C., 89

y

Yan, Martin, 103, 143
yogurt:
    apple-date breakfast, 51

yogurt *(cont.)*
    blueberry breakfast, 50
    fruit crunch, 166
    and mixed berries mold, 167
    and plums, 50

    potatoes, 130
    yum's, 166

zucchini, Sada's stuffed, 134
zwieback, 70-72